Design
Is How
It Works

DESIGN
IS HOW
IT WORKS

How the Smartest
Companies Turn
Products into Icons

JAY
GREENE

PORTFOLIO

PORTFOLIO PENGUIN
Published by the Penguin Group
Penguin Group (USA) Inc., 375 Hudson Street,
New York, New York 10014, U.S.A.
Penguin Group (Canada), 90 Eglinton Avenue East, Suite 700,
Toronto, Ontario, Canada M4P 2Y3
(a division of Pearson Penguin Canada Inc.)
Penguin Books Ltd, 80 Strand, London WC2R 0RL, England
Penguin Ireland, 25 St. Stephen's Green, Dublin 2, Ireland
(a division of Penguin Books Ltd)
Penguin Books Australia Ltd, 250 Camberwell Road, Camberwell,
Victoria 3124, Australia
(a division of Pearson Australia Group Pty Ltd)
Penguin Books India Pvt Ltd, 11 Community Centre, Panchsheel Park,
New Delhi – 110 017, India
Penguin Group (NZ), 67 Apollo Drive, Rosedale, North Shore 0632,
New Zealand (a division of Pearson New Zealand Ltd)
Penguin Books (South Africa) (Pty) Ltd, 24 Sturdee Avenue,
Rosebank, Johannesburg 2196, South Africa

Penguin Books Ltd, Registered Offices:
80 Strand, London WC2R 0RL, England

First published in 2010 by Portfolio Penguin,
a member of Penguin Group (USA) Inc.

10 9 8 7 6 5 4 3 2 1

Copyright © Jay Greene, 2010
All rights reserved

LIBRARY OF CONGRESS CATALOGING-IN-PUBLICATION DATA

Greene, Jay.
  Design is how it works : how the smartest companies turn products into icons /
Jay Greene.
    p. cm.
  Includes bibliographical references and index.
  ISBN 978-1-59184-322-1
  1. Industrial design—Case studies.   2. New products—Case studies.
3. Industrial design coordination.   4. Branding (Marketing)   I. Title.
  TS171.G726 2010
  658.5'752—dc22   2010004030

Printed in the United States of America
Set in ITC Galliard
Designed by Elyse Strongin, Neuwirth & Associates, Inc.

For Rochelle, Will, and Sam

Contents

Introduction

The winds along the west coast of Denmark are whipping up a froth on the fjord, spray shooting upward and dissipating in the cold afternoon air. Gray clouds fill the January sky. And although it isn't even five P.M. yet, darkness is quickly setting in.

I'm sitting in the passenger seat of Peter Petersen's Peugeot station wagon aboard a tiny ferry with enough room for only nine cars (as long as they're small). We're leaving Struer, where Petersen works as chief technical officer for the ultra-high-end consumer electronics maker Bang & Olufsen. In two minutes, we'll have made the four-hundred-meter journey across Venø Bugt, or Venø Bay, to the tiny island of Venø, where Petersen and about two hundred other people live. It's an isolated spot in an already remote region of Denmark, one of the key reasons Petersen likes it so much. As we make our way along the dark, narrow roads toward Petersen's home, his mobile phone rings. It's a work call that cuts out almost as quickly as Petersen answers it. "There's not much cell phone reception here," Petersen says, smiling. "That's one of the benefits of Venø."

Bang & Olufsen has long been one of the most innovative technology companies, a place where the cutting-edge design of its pencil-thin speakers matches their impeccable sound. But clouds have been gathering. For decades, the electronics maker built a loyal following among folks wealthy enough to shell out $4,750 for its BeoSound 9000 compact disc player or $20,000 for its BeoVision 9 plasma screen

Bang & Olufsen BeoSound 9000 compact disc player.
(Photo by Jesper Jørgen. Courtesy of Bang & Olufsen)

television. Sales, though, began to tank in 2008 as the objets d'art that the company sells stopped selling. In the fiscal year that ended just a few months after my visit with Petersen, B&O lost nearly $100 million.

It would be easy to blame the drop on the economy. After all, sales of all sorts of luxury goods plunged as the global recession spread. And no doubt that played a role. But B&O's problems run far deeper. The company had won over consumers for years with its gorgeous designs, so stunning that several, such as its 1969 Beogram 1200 record player and its 1989 Beocord VX 5000 videocassette recorder, are part of the Museum of Modern Art's (MoMA) permanent collection. But as B&O learned all too painfully, design isn't merely making something beautiful.

Back in 2003, the *New York Times*'s wonderful "Consumed" columnist Rob Walker examined the birth of Apple's iPod, explaining how it became more than just a nifty consumer electronics gadget, but a cultural phenomenon. "Most people make the mistake of thinking design is what it looks like," Apple CEO Steve Jobs told Walker. "People think it's this veneer—that the designers are handed this box and told, 'Make it look good!' That's not what we think design is. It's not just what it looks like and feels like. Design is how it works."

For most of Bang & Olufsen's life, which began in 1925, making high-quality audio and video devices look stunning was enough. Once consumers turned on their B&O television, radio, or stereo, they could forget about it and just watch or listen. The sound and picture quality were first-rate. Even when the devices were turned off, they spoke volumes

3

with their lustrous materials and considered craftsmanship. Company executives like to joke that B&O customers stare at their televisions even when they are off. For decades, that strategy allowed Bang & Olufsen to thrive.

Indeed, when I first met Petersen two years earlier, Bang & Olufsen was a model of success. The location of our meeting couldn't have been any farther removed from Venø. We chatted in a luxury suite at the Venetian Hotel in Las Vegas during the Consumer Electronics Show, the annual gadget-fest that brings some 140,000 manufacturers, retailers, analysts, and journalists to Sin City. It's a convention I've attended for the better part of a decade, working as a reporter writing about technology and design at *BusinessWeek* magazine. And just like the casino that night, Bang & Olufsen was brimming with success. Operating profits that year grew 22 percent.

During our conversation, Petersen described B&O's design process, and it was unlike any I'd ever heard of. The company, he told me, doesn't have a single designer on staff. Instead, it contracts with freelance designers in order to keep them entirely removed from corporate politics and bureaucracy. The company goes a step further, giving designers complete control, even allowing them to kill a product if it doesn't meet their design objectives. "We don't design for manufacturing," Petersen told me that night in Las Vegas. "We manufacture for design."

It struck me as an entirely novel approach to creating products. The company handed off designs to a few geniuses, who then worked their craft behind a black curtain. Those designers trusted their instincts, not marketing reports or finance dicta, to make products that turned customers into loyal patrons. The high-end approach allowed the minnow that is B&O to survive in a sea of sharks with names like Sony, Samsung, Panasonic, and Philips.

But the ecosystem was changing, and B&O didn't keep up. In 2002, B&O launched a portable music player, the $460 BeoSound 2, just a few months after the first iPod hit store shelves. It was breathtaking, a polished stainless-steel disk that fit in the palm of your hand. But it had one big problem: no screen. Back then, users downloaded songs onto a tiny flash card that could hold about fifty tunes, a small enough number that navigation was relatively easy. But B&O designers didn't appreciate that the capacity of those cards would quickly grow to the point where they could hold thousands of songs. Use one of those cards and it became nearly impossible to navigate to that one song you really wanted to hear. (Interestingly, Apple managed to avoid the problem with its iPod shuffle by making the device just one in a family of products, targeted primarily at athletes willing to trade off navigation for size.)

A few years later, B&O debuted its Serene mobile phone, an eye-catching masterpiece that when opened resembled a bird in flight. The phone, which sold for $1,275, had a tiny motor in it that peeled the phone open for use. The keypad was a circle of digits, evoking a rotary dial. A work of beauty, except that the rotary keypad made texting—a mandatory feature in the digital age—a challenge. And forget about trying to type an e-mail.

As technology evolved, consumers demanded more control. Great design meant creating gadgets that allowed users to easily choose a song and play it on any device without

5

having to race to the user's manual to figure out how. And that will continue to evolve to televisions, where users will want to start watching recorded programs on the set in the living room and finish watching in the bedroom. It requires manufacturers such as Bang & Olufsen to have the software expertise to make the tasks easy for consumers. "Today, quality has a different meaning," says B&O's director of design and concepts, Flemming Møller Pedersen. "We believed a little too long in the old values, in the old meaning of quality."

The world B&O clung to is the one created by Walter Gropius and the disciples of the Bauhaus movement in the first part of the twentieth century. As the world entered the machine age, Gropius launched the Bauhaus school to bring design theory to the industrial process. It championed streamlined and utilitarian design in mass production, and fostered the concept that the form of an object should follow its function. And even though the school itself was pressured out of existence by the Nazis after just fourteen years, the movement, which spawned angular buildings designed by Ludwig Mies van der Rohe, minimalist chairs by Marcel Breuer, and sleek lamps by Marianne Brandt, has never waned. You still see its influence in stores such as IKEA, chairs from Herman Miller, and kitchen goods from Bodum.

But effective design in the twenty-first century goes well beyond creating an object that might one day go on display at MoMA. Design isn't merely about making products aesthetically beautiful. Design today is about creating experiences that consumers crave. The look and feel of a product is table stakes—it can forge the beginning of an emotional bond with customers. The best products and services must deliver singular experiences unobtainable anywhere else. The smartest designs address needs consumers never knew they had. If you traveled back in time a few years, you'd be hard-pressed to find many consumers clamoring for a device that would let them make calls, play games, check the weather, read newspapers, and purchase auction items all on a gizmo that would fit in a pants pocket. But when Apple delivered the iPhone, it altered the dynamics of the mobile phone industry.

If there was ever a company to make the case that the best design is about creating great experiences, it's Apple. Forests have been felled to publish the thousands of books, magazine articles, and newspaper clippings to chronicle the Cupertino, California, company's success. Apple made cute computers

7

for an elite bunch for years, until it exploded onto the mainstream consumer consciousness with the iPod. The portable digital music player didn't do anything that several other rival devices weren't already doing. It just did it better. A lot better. Apple created a gorgeous device that seamlessly connected to a music store offering easy access to more tunes than any consumer could ever hope to hear.

Consumers took notice as far back as 1998, when Apple launched its candy-colored iMac G3 line of computers, even if few bought them. With the iPod, and the subsequent creation of the iPhone and its sleek line of MacBook laptop computers, Apple has become the poster child for design. Every company, every design consultant, every journalist holds Apple up as the model. Rather than racing to the bottom, cutting costs to eke out modest earnings while edging out competitors, Apple went in the other direction. It spent more money designing a series of gadgets consumers loved. And because they were smitten, those consumers were willing to pay a premium over the other somewhat similar gadgets on the store shelves nearby. Apple's earnings soared. It became one of the most admired brands on the face of the earth.

No wonder, then, that so many companies want to follow in Apple's footsteps. "I can't tell you how many product briefs we get saying we want a product that's as good or better than the iPhone," says John Barratt. He's the president and CEO of Teague, the Seattle design studio founded in 1926 by legendary designer Walter Dorwin Teague, who created Eastman Kodak's Brownie cameras. Barratt's clients include Boeing, Microsoft, and Samsung, among others.

When we chat over lunch at the café at the Seattle Art

Museum's outdoor sculpture garden just a few blocks from Teague's headquarters, Barratt, a Brit, is sporting the modern designer's uniform: stylish silver glasses, black button-down shirt, black slacks, and a pair of black casual shoes. He rolls his eyes at the request to one-up the iPhone. "That's a five-alarm brief for me," Barratt continues. "Those folks just don't get it. An iPhone is not a product. It's a manifestation of a culture."

It starts with Jobs and Apple's senior vice president of industrial design, Jonathan Ive, two executives with an appreciation and understanding of design that goes well beyond what's common in the corner offices of Corporate America. When the company developed the first iPod, the one that these days looks almost Jurassic, with its scroll wheel, a button in the center, and four more beneath its LCD screen, the pair started with an overriding goal—keep things simple for users. Other companies talk a good game about developing great user experiences. But then they let marketing staff add features that make products confusing. They allow engineers to alter designs in ways that make products complex. That's not Apple's approach.

Executives, analysts, and consultants have pored over Apple's design strategy, deconstructing it and then reconstituting it to apply to their needs. They've come up with design matrices, flowcharts, and playbooks all intended to replicate Apple's process and capture some of its success. But there are few companies that can actually succeed in mimicking Apple. Partly, that's because of the culture that Barratt mentions. Then there are the vagaries of the consumer electronics market. There's Apple's competition, companies such as

9

Microsoft, which let Apple establish a beachhead in markets where it later tried to compete. And, of course, there's Jobs and Ive.

As brilliant as Apple is, though, it's not the only company that's been able to ride great design to economic heights. And the others have taken entirely different paths from Apple's. There's a common thread: Doing consistently great design requires a commitment to it.

That's a challenge for a lot of CEOs, many of whom rose through the ranks in corporate finance departments. They often view design as an additional cost, not an increase in value. What's more, design isn't something companies can benchmark. "There isn't a McKinsey-type guy you can bring in," says David Merkoski, executive creative director at frog design, another leading design firm, founded in 1969 by Hartmut Esslinger, who went on to codesign Apple's "Snow White" computers in the 1980s. The company has since worked on everything from Hewlett-Packard's TouchSmart touch-screen PCs to irons made by golf industry giant Titleist. Merkoski, with a thick mop of brown hair and matching mustache and beard, finds many executives unnerved by the guesswork of design. "Design is an argument," Merkoski continues. "You can't prove it. There are no metrics to it."

That's why executives frequently acknowledge the importance of using design to create great user experience but all too often deliver complex products and services that leave customers disinterested or even frustrated. Their companies often resort to improving existing products rather than creating entirely new ones. They can measure existing markets. They know which company has what share. But the design

10

breakthroughs are often huge leaps from existing products. Their creators take daring chances and challenge convention, something Merkoski calls "conceptual hallucination." It's the kind of language that unnerves numbers-driven executives. But companies need to take those sorts of informed risks if they are going to have a chance at achieving greatness. "All of us, before we got the Jesus phone"—what he and plenty of others call the iPhone—"didn't know what was possible."

It would be wrong to blame a lack of ingenuity on finance-bred executives alone. Designers themselves often speak in a language only they understand, rather than make it easy for the uninitiated to learn how they work. They use words such as *empathy, authenticity, ideation, singularity,* and *simplicity,* words that outside the design-world echo chamber are broad to the point of meaninglessness.

Those parallel worlds are the ones I hope to bridge in this book. I'll use some of those words, explaining the concepts, because they're too important to dismiss. Too often, executives shy away from spending money on design because they don't understand the benefits and they don't trust the folks who can deliver it. And too often, designers do themselves no favors by staying in the vacuum of their own world, alienating outsiders when business, more than ever, needs them to make the experience of using products and services more enjoyable.

Let's demystify design. First, it's important to understand that design, at least the way I'm using the term, isn't merely about style and form. Those are important. But design is really about the way products and services come to life. The companies that build the most enduring relationships with customers often do so by creating an environment where design flourishes. They have leadership that embraces design, executives who trust their gut and their employees as much as they trust all the data they receive about their business. To really grasp design is to intuit what customers want, often before customers even know they want it. That's not something you can learn in a focus group or an online survey.

It comes from truly understanding customers. The companies in this book often do this instinctively because, as you'll read, they launched their businesses to fulfill their own unmet needs, companies such as Clif Bar, Ace Hotels, and Virgin Atlantic. They remain extreme users—the most demanding customers who can verbalize exactly what they want. But there are plenty of design-centric companies that are virtual anthropologists, who do deep ethnographic research on customers, companies such as Nike and LEGO. They observe the people who use their products, trying to figure out where the next breakthrough is even if those customers can't quite envision it. Design may seem like a lofty discipline, but the companies in this book show that it succeeds only with real-world observation.

In a business world that increasingly rewards differentiation, consistently great design can't be achieved through lip service. To succeed, companies need to rethink their innovation process and even their organizational structure. Designers need to participate in the earliest stages of product development, rather than get called in at the end to put a fancy gloss on a new product just before it goes to market.

12

They need to work hand in hand with engineers at the beginning of the process, and with marketers at the end.

You'll also see that the most successful companies in this book are often led by CEOs who are willing to cede control, even ones who are willing to feel a bit out of control. It's something that frog design's chief creative officer, Mark Rolston, refers to as the "coarse process" of design. Often, it's not pretty. You need to feel your way through the process, not aim at a predetermined end point. Mistakes get made. Decisions get revisited. But that's really the only way to improve the product. "You don't know exactly where you're headed. You arrive at something," Rolston says. You can't throw good business practices out the window. But the best companies spend less time worrying about risk mitigation—avoiding cost overruns, blown timetables—than they do on figuring out how to embrace risk support.

And forget about design being important just to companies that make shiny objects. Smart companies are applying the lessons of great design to create products and services that will never grace the walls of MoMA. "Classically, we have design being about stuff," says Tim Brown, who runs IDEO, the Palo Alto, California, design firm that's at the forefront of a movement that uses the lessons of design to set a management strategy. "It used to be, 'We have this technology, wrap it nicely.'" But Brown and his colleagues at IDEO realized that the approach designers use to create new products had wider applications. They helped pioneer the notion, dubbed Design Thinking, that design could revolutionize development of products and services, even in businesses where aesthetics aren't particularly important.

13

IDEO uses anthropology, sociology, and psychology to help all sorts of companies learn how they can make experiences better for customers. It teaches companies how to create a process that is constantly learning about the people who use their products. These days, you'll find IDEO working with the Transportation Security Administration to improve the experience of passing through airport security. And you'll see the firm working with Sloan-Kettering Cancer Center to make its chemotherapy process—everything from waiting for doctors to administering drugs—easier. "For me, design is about answering so many questions other than what the form of the thing should be," Brown says. "It's about creating new choices, not just choosing from things that already exist."

The companies you'll read about in the subsequent pages aren't the eight best companies at design. (That might be a very different list.) They are all companies that do design and often use Design Thinking really well. But my goal was to pick companies of different sizes, in different businesses, and in different locations. I selected old and young alike. Publicly traded and privately held. Design is something at which any company can succeed. And the companies that embrace the idea that design is about creating a great experience are the ones that will flourish in the twenty-first century.

A few years ago, Bang & Olufsen could have been one of these companies. And maybe it will rise again. Back in Petersen's efficient Danish home on Venø, he's talking about his real passion, blues music. We're sitting on Petersen's red suede sofa in a den framed from floor to wall to ceiling in the blond woods common throughout Denmark. Petersen gives his new toy, a BeoSound 5, a whirl. The company just

14

launched the product, a six-thousand-dollar digital audio jukebox, a few weeks before my visit. The centerpiece is a 10.4-inch LCD display with a meaty aluminum wheel on the right side to navigate through your music library. When you land on a song, the album art pops up on the screen.

Petersen turns the dial to zip through his tunes, stopping at John Lee Hooker, then Robert Cray and Robert Johnson, playing a sample of each. And he takes joy in introducing me to Danish blues bands. First it's the Bayous, Danes with a Cajun twang. Then it's Dan Klarskov & the Honeydrippers, and then Johnny Madsen, who sings "Langerhuse Blues," an ode to his hometown, in Danish. The fit and finish of the BeoSound 5 is striking, but Petersen revels in sharing the details of his favorite music.

The company is trying to figure out how to please customers who want more than just a beautiful product. They want a great experience. The BeoSound 5 may not be the answer, but it's a step in the right direction. "Bang & Olufsen still offers the chance to do the things I believe in. We go search for things like this," Petersen says, as he flips through music on his BeoSound 5. "We are obliged to. That is the essence of Bang & Olufsen." It's a path that the smartest companies are traveling.

15

1

PORSCHE

Incongruities abound. Thanksgiving is a week away, and Christmas just around the corner. I realize that Los Angeles, a place where I lived for nearly a decade, is always warmer than most of the United States. But today seems absurd. Oversize Christmas baubles and garlands decorate the streets of Beverly Hills. And I'm sweating as the thermometer tops 80 degrees. I decide my sport coat has to go.

I'm dressed up to attend press briefings in advance of the 2008 Los Angeles Auto Show. Foreign carmakers dominate the proceedings. BMW debuts its environmentally imaginative MINI E concept car, a vehicle it will lease over the coming months to five hundred Americans to test a new electric battery. Ferrari gives its drop-dead sexy California, a front-engine V-8 hardtop convertible, a U.S. premiere. And Nissan rolls out its perky Cube, a bit of a knockoff of the Scion xB perhaps, but a fun little SUV nonetheless.

Meanwhile, in a conference room at the U.S. Capitol, the wan, glum CEOs of the Big Three U.S. automakers beg senators to bail out their companies, victims of crushing cost structures, oppressive dealer agreements, and, perhaps most sadly of all, the very same executives' inability to innovate. No place was that more evident than on the floor of the auto show, where the unimaginative offerings from those carmakers stood in stark contrast to the unbridled creativity of their international rivals.

Sport coat in the car, I make my way to Petree Hall, the cavernous showroom at the convention center that German luxury carmaker Porsche has all to itself. There's little lack of creativity in this room. On the main stage are the new models Porsche chose to highlight at the show—sporty versions of its entry-level roadsters, the Boxster S and the Cayman S. They're zippy little two-seaters that let you know the second you look at them that they're Porsches. They both have the signature trapezoid-shaped hood, the big air intakes below the headlamps, and the superlow clearance from the ground, more common in race cars than street vehicles.

And what makes that so identifiably Porsche? The answer lies in the car that sits between the other two models. It's the Gmünd Porsche 356-001, the very first car built with the Porsche nameplate. The 1948 creation of Ferry Porsche, who founded the company with his father Ferdinand, is a gray two-seater, squat like every Porsche since. It has the telltale curves over the wheels and around the fenders that anyone who's lusted after a Porsche can identify instantly. It's a car that looks like it would be a blast to take for a spin along the California coast. "It's still clearly the inspiration for

20

Gmünd Porsche 356-001. *(© 2010 Porsche AG)*

all our cars," says Klaus Berning, a member of Porsche's six-person executive board and head of sales and marketing for the company, during the company's press conference. While it's hardly the Boxster or Cayman, it's easy to see how those cars—built six decades later—share its heritage.

During the presentation, the company plays a video, shot some fifteen or twenty years earlier, of Ferry Porsche

21

discussing the fundamental traits that define his company. "Independence has always been the attitude at Porsche, to do not what is expected, but what we feel is right," says the aging founder, who died in 1998. "It is said, I believe, that so many creations today are just like all the rest. This is why Porsche must remain small and independent. Without independence, without the freedom to try new ideas, the world will not move ahead, but live in fear of its own potential." And that's why, Porsche goes on, his company will never vet its ideas with the masses and let smaller minds crush its ingenuity. "Committees lead to creations that have no soul, no clear identity," Porsche says. "This is why no Porsche will ever be created by a committee, but by a handful of people inside these walls who know what a Porsche is."

It's almost eerie hearing Ferry Porsche's design maxims from the grave. These days, plenty of executives see design as the new black in management strategy. Those who get it talk about giving designers the freedom to make mistakes and bemoan the problem of "focus-grouping an idea to death" as though they were the first to think of it. And here's a gray, slow-speaking Porsche, in the winter of his life, using the same language, conveying the same ideas, decades earlier.

Don't make the mistake that design at Porsche is all about looks. Its cars are gorgeous, no doubt. But for Porsche, design is also about authenticity. That's an overused word in the corner offices of most corporate headquarters. But in Porsche's case, it's a word that had resonance in the earliest days of the company. When Ferry Porsche was asked about the design of the 356, he said, "In the beginning, I looked around but couldn't find the car I dreamt of, so I decided to build it myself." The son of a car designer—his father Ferdinand created the original Volkswagen Beetle at the request of Adolf Hitler—Porsche infused his company with a passion for creating dream-worthy vehicles that continues to this day. It's the reason J.D. Power and Associates ranked Porsche in 2008 not just the top automaker in quality but also in delighting customers with design and performance.

So what does design authenticity mean? There have been books written about it, such as James H. Gilmore and B. Joseph Pine II's *Authenticity: What Consumers Really Want.* Their argument is that consumers respond to products and services that are "real." Customers are willing to shell out money for goods that engage them, goods to which they have personal connections. The way a company such as Porsche creates those products is by developing cars that its designers crave. No cutting corners. Nothing inauthentic that risks the company's credibility. From that first 356, Porsche's strategy has been to create cars that its designers wish they could own.

That's one reason Porsches have evolved from modes of transportation to mythic symbols. Its fans don't just drive the cars; they collect them. The company believes that roughly 70 percent of all Porsches built since the original 356 are still on the road today. With that lust come the scores of Porsche coffee table books stuffed with glossy photos of its race cars, its 356s, and its 911s. Porsche clubs circle the globe, from the United States to Germany to New Zealand to Lebanon. Porsche has used design to create a cult.

Think about Porsche's business model for a second. It has used design to create a feel, an intangible emotion about its cars that allows it to charge a significant premium. That feel

23

is what makes its customers passionate about Porsche. None of this was created haphazardly. Porsche designers from Ferry Porsche to the people who make its cars today are deeply engaged in the auto industry. They love cars. And Porsche has given them the tools and the latitude to create products that spark their passion. The premise is that if Porsche designers love their products, customers will follow.

One other important piece of Porsche's strategy to consider: It's not trying to appeal to everyone. As you'll see, Porsche works hard in each of its four model groups to appeal to the needs and desires of specific niches in its market. It's not trying to create an alternative to the Honda Accord or the Ford Focus, mass-market cars that work just fine but don't inspire the sort of passion that allows Porsche to charge its premium. The company is focused on well-off buyers who crave cars that have that mythic quality that Porsche has been able to forge over the decades.

I've never owned a Porsche, so I decided to learn firsthand what it is to experience driving one. Two months after the Los Angeles Auto Show, I pay a visit to Porsche's test track in Leipzig, Germany. The warmth of Los Angeles is a distant memory with the late January temperatures in this former East German city hovering just above freezing. There's a slight dusting of snow still sprinkling the fields nearby. I'm behind the steering wheel of a Porsche 911 Carrera S, a souped-up version of an already souped-up car that would cost about $100,000 at a United States dealership. The 385-horsepower engine can push this little dynamo from 0 to 60

24

miles per hour in 4.3 seconds. It uses the new 7-speed Porsche Doppelkupplung—known among non-German speakers as PDK—an automated manual transmission system that the company has built into its race cars for nearly two decades, providing quick gearshifts with no loss of power.

Sitting next to me is Guido Majewski, an eleven-year racing veteran who now works full-time teaching race driving. He works here to give Porsche customers and would-be customers the opportunity to do things they'd never do on the street. Like trying to go from 0 to 60 miles per hour in 4.3 seconds.

2009 Porsche 911 Carrera S. *(© Stefan Warter/Porsche AG)*

PORSCHE

The track covers 2.3 miles and is built with ten different corners, curves, and chicanes that replicate some of the most famous twists in auto racing. I zip over the Laguna Seca Corkscrew, an undulating right-left-right combination taken from a track in Monterey, California, that drops me onto a long straightaway where I push the Carrera north of 80 miles per hour before hitting the brakes to manage the deceptively tricky Mobil 1 S turn from Nürburgring, the legendary track just a few hours south of Leipzig. Majewski is telling me to brake earlier so I can carry just the right amount of speed into the first right turn before hitting the gas to achieve maximum speed out of the left turn that's approaching. Instead, I'm braking in the corner, which means the car needs much more pop coming out. It's not efficient and it cuts my speed.

After eight laps, I get out of the car. My hands are shaking a bit and I feel woozy, like I rode a roller coaster just a bit too long. Even though it's 35 degrees on this gray morning, I'm dripping with sweat. And I'm beaming. "I recognize that smile," Majewski says. "It's the same one that our customers have when they do this." Then Majewski, a gracious and patient man with graying hair and a firm handshake, takes me for a spin, driving the track the way it's supposed to be driven.

Turns out my trip over the Corkscrew is like a drive to the mall compared to the line and speed taken by Majewski. And as he approaches the Mobil 1 S, he slams the brakes before the right turn, starts twisting the steering wheel to the right so that the rear of the car drifts out ever so slightly to the left, putting him in perfect position to pull the same maneuver in the opposite direction on the left turn. In an instant, we're approaching 100 miles per hour again. I comment that most

26

Carrera owners have never done that and wouldn't even know how.

"It's a pity," Majewski says.

Maybe, I think. But for Porsche, the point of the 911, the highest-performance car among its production stable, is that it can do all that a driver like Majewski asks of it, even if most drivers will never push their cars nearly that hard. Porsche cars are designed for driving, not merely looking good in the driveway. Porsche marketing chief Berning tells me, "We have a saying in German: We want to make sure the worm is tasty for the fish, and not the fisherman." I'm sure that's lost something in the translation. But the point he is making is that Porsche design starts with authenticity. Its cars can do everything that their sporty appearance conveys.

When Porsche approaches design, everything begins with the 911. The iconic rear-engine car, which first debuted at the Frankfurt Motor Show in 1963, remains one of the most durable franchises in automotive history. Over the years, Porsche has tweaked the design, making the car slightly wider and longer. But the basic look has never veered. "If you go back in the history of the company, the 911 plays a very important role," says Porsche design chief Michael Mauer. "It is the center of our brand."

I'm talking with Mauer, a lean man with a full head of dirty-blond hair, at Porsche's headquarters in the Zuffenhausen district of Stuttgart, Germany. As Mauer describes Porsche's design DNA, he grabs a piece of paper and a pen and starts sketching. "You need certain elements that make a Porsche look like a Porsche," Mauer says. The pen moves quickly over the paper. Engines need air to cool them; Porsche

27

always uses intakes instead of a radiator grill. He scribbles some intakes. The cabin of the car always tapers to the rear, which creates "a strong shoulder," Mauer says, sketching lines from the front to the rear of the car. To convey the power of Porsche's engine, the rims on the wheels are always open, making the brake calipers visible. And perhaps the most telltale Porsche design cue of all—the fenders around the front headlamps are always higher than the hood. Mauer wasn't trying to draw a specific car, just one that has Porsche DNA in it. But the car he's sketched is about as close to a 911 as you could get.

There is distinct Porsche styling in the interiors of its cars too. The ignition switch is always on the left side of the steering column. Porsche enthusiasts know that dates back to the early days of racing, when drivers lined their cars up along the pit walls in the order in which they qualified. When the start flag dropped, drivers would run across the track to their cars, key in hand, to start their engines and begin racing. Porsche engineers figured it would save time to start the car with the left hand while the right hand put the transmission in gear. It's kept the location of the ignition switch ever since.

Another interior styling point: The dashboard instrumentation is laid out vertically. That's because Porsche's sports cars are lower to the ground than most models, leaving less interior room in the car. A horizontal dash just wouldn't fit in its two-seaters. And because the new, bigger cars take their styling cues from the 911, they too have narrow, vertical dashboards. "You will be able to enter any Porsche with closed eyes and identify once you are inside that this is a Porsche," says Porsche's executive vice president for research and

28

development, Wolfgang Dürheimer. Porsche even designs the sound of its cars, everything from the engine roar to the thud of its doors closing. "Nothing of this comes by accident," Dürheimer says. That's because Porsche has a sound lab at the Porsche Research & Development Centre in Weissach, Germany, where different audible possibilities are tested. The company's acoustic engineers don't just work to eliminate rattles and squeaks. They test vehicles in an anechoic chamber, where they can tweak fan placement or water cooling systems to come up with the engine sound they want.

Porsche starts the design process on new models, and refreshes existing ones, with a competition. As many as five designers come to Mauer, each with five different ideas for a car, sketched out in detail. Mauer guides them, picking the best of the bunch from each designer, making sure that each car is different enough from the versions he's selected from the other designers to ensure variety. The designers then refine their ideas and build models, roughly three feet long. "Sometimes it works as a sketch, but not in the third dimension," Mauer said. So the designers go back and rework their concepts.

From there, Mauer and Porsche's six-member executive board pick the two best designs to turn into full-scale models. The designers whose ideas were rejected are given a week or two to lick their wounds. Then they work on the teams of the designers whose concepts advanced, because no one designer can manage all the details of creating a new model. "Some of them are deeply frustrated. It's your baby and someone is telling you that your baby isn't good-looking enough," Mauer says. "I always tell young designers that part of their salary is for pain and suffering."

29

At the same time, designers wrestle with engineers, who push for the most aerodynamic vehicle possible. "The designers and the aerodynamics guys are always in a hustle," Dürheimer says. Designers wanted a rounded front end on the Cayman, even though engineers showed that a square front works better from an aerodynamics perspective. "It kills the visual message," says Dürheimer, an engineer himself. Designers won. But he pushes to get designers out of their studios, where real-world challenges rarely interfere with their creativity. "They don't like to walk into a wind tunnel," Dürheimer says of designers. "A wind tunnel atmosphere isn't creative." But he pushes to bring them there to help designers understand the impact of their flourishes. Whoever wins, however, those debates are critical to arriving at the best product. "When we develop a new car, we have a lot of this because everyone wants to be a champion," Dürheimer says.

The one thing Porsche never does is seek out voices outside the company to decide the look of its cars. It never puts concept vehicles in front of consumers to test ideas. "When it comes to design, it is not a democratic process," sales and marketing chief Berning says. "You can't do market research on design." The executive board has final say. That board, on which Berning and Dürheimer both sit, is the keeper of Ferry Porsche's vision. Its members are the "handful of people inside these walls who know what a Porsche is."

Take the Porsche Cayenne. It is, without question, the biggest design challenge Porsche has ever faced. The company wanted to grow its business beyond its traditional sports-car line. All those visual cues, those powerful engine sounds, everything that defined what it is to be a Porsche, evolved

30

from the 356 and the 911. All together, they comprised the world's most recognized two-door sports car. Porsche had to figure out how to make the Cayenne be both a Porsche and an SUV at the same time. How did the company do it? Design.

It wasn't easy, and few Porsche-philes gave the company a free pass. Auto reviewers, almost to a person, hated the sports utility vehicle when Porsche unveiled it at the Paris Auto

2010 Porsche Cayenne GTS Porsche Design Edition.
(© 2010 Porsche AG)

Show in 2002. To most of them, the Cayenne didn't meet their expectations of what a Porsche should be, namely a two-door speedster with the low, rounded look of virtually every other Porsche up until that time. "I have seen more attractive gangrenous wounds than this," sniped Jeremy Clarkson, one of the hosts of the popular and influential British car show *Top Gear*, in his review. "It has the sex appeal of a camel with gingivitis."

But Porsche executives, frustrated that its customers were turning to rivals such as Mercedes-Benz and BMW for family vehicles, knew better. Designers used themes from the 911—the fenders higher than the hood, for example. But they also knew that reviewers—the people who love the 911—would initially pan the Cayenne. "Sometimes you need some time to understand what is a good design," Dürheimer says.

Not only has the Cayenne sold better than every other Porsche model since its 2003 debut, but it didn't diminish the sportiness of the brand. To the contrary, sales of the 911, the Boxster, and the Cayman grew every year following the Cayenne's introduction, until the financial crisis hit in 2008. It helped turn Porsche, prior to the global economic collapse, into the most profitable carmaker in the world. And the Cayenne gave Porsche the financial breathing room to continue to design great sports cars. "If we would have followed the public opinion, we wouldn't have made an SUV," Dürheimer says.

So why has the Cayenne been successful? Sure, it's fast, like every Porsche. I took a Cayenne GTS out on the Autobahn, the German highway system famous for stretches with no speed limit, and put it in sport mode, where the body lowers nearly an inch below its normal setting and the suspension stiffens. In no time, I was clocking 130 miles per hour, plenty fast for me, though the Cayenne still had another 35 miles per hour or so in it.

The Cayenne is one of the most capable off-road SUVs on the market. Most of its rivals, such as the BMW X5 and Mercedes-Benz GL, are designed with the idea that most of their SUV customers will never take their pricey vehicles off-road. They're zippy, stylish rides, meant for cruising around town or on the freeway. Porsche, though, went in a different direction. With a flick of a switch on the center console, an air suspension system increases ground clearance for those times you need to drive over a bunch of logs. The Cayenne includes a traction system that determines the optimum power split among the wheels, depending on conditions. And it uses computer-controlled hydraulics to offset body roll when the car corners sharply.

Maybe the most fun feature to play with is Porsche Hill Control. Back in Leipzig, I give it a go on Porsche's off-road circuit, a 3.7-mile track on a former military training ground adjacent to the test track. As I slowly crawl up a hill with a 60 percent grade, my driving teacher Majewski tells me to take my foot off the gas. I oblige, slipping my foot over to the brake pedal. Then Majewski tells me to take my foot off the brake too. On its own, the car just stops. We turn around and go back down the same steep hill and Majewski tells me to release the gas and brake again. The Cayenne takes over, easing me effortlessly down to the bottom of the hill. Not too many Cayenne owners are going to take their SUVs— which when loaded with goodies can top $100,000—on such an expedition. But they could.

And that's the key to Porsche design. Think about Majewski's spin around the Leipzig track in the 911. He drove the car harder than the vast majority of Porsche owners, and it responded perfectly. The Cayenne eagerly tackles hills steeper than those on which most owners would ever think to take their expensive SUVs. But when Porsche owners push their cars to handle the most challenging roads, the vehicles do so almost instinctively. The company's cars don't merely look good; they perform impeccably. It's not just a look that Porsche customers desire; it's an experience.

The success of the Cayenne has Porsche pushing even further beyond its two-seat sports-car roots with the four-door Panamera, which hit showroom floors in September 2009. Berning says the company applied much of what it learned from the development of the Cayenne in developing the Panamera. That experience helped Porsche recognize the need to move beyond two-seaters while meeting customers' expectations of Porsche performance. "We get older and our customers get older," Berning says. The average age of a 911 owner is fifty. But Berning is quick to add that Porsche isn't merely trying to hold on to its existing customers. "It is all about attracting new customers to the brand, and keeping them loyal," Berning says.

In developing the Panamera, Porsche again looked inside its walls for design. "We know how a Porsche should drive. So we didn't ask anybody," Berning says. "The way the car drives, smells, sounds, and feels. We know what it should be." The company did invest heavily in market research after it designed the car—more so with the Panamera than with any other car before. But it showed the car to focus groups only

34

to think about how to market it. Customers knew the car could perform. The trait they didn't pick up on was the functionality—the ability to stash golf clubs or to fit several bags of groceries, something that's more than a bit of a challenge with every other Porsche save the Cayenne. "We found that the functionality had to be underlined more," Berning says.

While I visited Germany, Porsche was in the midst of a brash attempt to use the financial strength afforded by the Cayenne's success to seize control of Europe's largest automaker, Volkswagen. The idea was to own Volkswagen, which makes the frame and doors for the Cayenne, lest the company fall into a rival's hands. So Porsche accumulated stock and options worth nearly 75 percent of Volkswagen, taking out billions in loans to acquire the ever-dwindling number of shares left.

When the credit crisis hit a few months later, Porsche's acquisition dreams evaporated. It was trapped in a credit squeeze, forcing it to pay down debt with money it didn't have. Porsche went from predator to prey. By the end of the summer, the company's cherished independence was all but gone. Instead of owning Volkswagen, Porsche agreed to be acquired by the company, becoming one of ten brands in a stable that includes Audi, Bentley, Bugatti, and Lamborghini. Porsche's chief executive and chief financial officers, who engineered the overreaching acquisition bid, both resigned as a result.

Will Porsche, under new ownership, remain independent? Will its design process be subject to new directives from Volkswagen's Wolfsburg headquarters? Will Porsche have the freedom to try new ideas, as Ferry Porsche once preached, or will it live in fear of its own potential?

In the aftermath of the news, Volkswagen said the right things. "Porsche's independence in the integrated group will be safeguarded, in line with Volkswagen's proven decentralized management model," the company said when it announced the deal. "As is the case today with Audi and other successful group brands, Porsche will retain its identity, while at the same time benefiting from its membership in the integrated group." That seems to acknowledge the importance of Porsche's design culture.

It's not what Ferry Porsche had in mind. But given the financial turmoil caused by the misguided acquisition attempt, which led some to question Porsche's ability to survive, it may be the best Porsche fans can hope for.

2

NIKE

Mark Parker doesn't have an office as much as he does a museum. It's no MoMA, mind you. But the collection of artwork, sports memorabilia, and pop-culture artifacts crammed into the relatively modest chief executive suite at Nike is almost overwhelming to a first-time visitor.

Start with the two huge portraits by German painter Sebastian Kruger hanging behind his desk. One is an oversize visage of the craggy-faced Rolling Stones guitarist Keith Richards, who looks as though he's peering over Parker's shoulder as the latter reads e-mail, writes memos, and plots Nike strategy. The other shows Jimi Hendrix, eyes shut, focused on a guitar solo. Nearby, there's a playful sculpture by Japanese artist Jun Goshima, where he's assembled bones in the shape of Nike's Dunk basketball shoes, as if archaeologists unearthed the treasure and unlocked the mystery of prehistoric sneaker making.

The desk itself is a glass-covered case with dozens upon

dozens of curios inside—items such as the checklist Apollo 15 commander Dave Scott, the seventh person to walk on the moon and the first to drive on it, carried with him on the lunar surface. As for the blond-wood bookshelves on either side of his desk, they hold no books at all. One shelf is loaded with a collection of robots. Another is stocked with toy rocket ships. This being Nike, there are sports memorabilia too, such as the Trek TTX time-trial bike behind the sofa I'm sitting on, a bike once used by Nike athlete Lance Armstrong.

Parker's office says a lot about the approach to design at Nike these days. This is a company that has remained surprisingly relevant nearly a half century into its life, despite constant challenges over the years from giant rivals such as Adidas and a never-ending stream of niche competitors, such as L.A. Gear in the late 1980s or D.C. Shoes today. And it's done so by turning its design eye toward modern culture, pushing way beyond its roots as a performance running-shoe company. The lesson Nike teaches is to evolve through design, finding new markets and new opportunities for growth, regardless of size or even success.

Nike began that life as a company that made high-performance track shoes for world-class athletes. It made the sneakers worn by Steve Prefontaine and Joan Benoit Samuelson as they set world track-and-field records in the 1970s and 1980s. And while Nike still shoes many of the world's most talented athletes, it has evolved into a company that's just as adept at selling fashion sneakers, shirts, and all sorts of other apparel to the rest of us.

Remaining hip and managing to stay on the cutting edge of sports technology is an astonishing feat for a company that's often dismissed as a corporate behemoth, too big to appreciate the nuances of the various markets in which it plays. But Nike has managed to be the shoe of choice for both world-record-holding marathoners and skateboard punks, the shirt of choice for both World Cup soccer players and overweight soccer dads. And its company culture has evolved to one that appreciates social trends beyond the track oval, the baseball diamond, and the basketball court.

Parker, a legendary Nike designer who joined the company in 1979, sets that agenda. He's the guy who helped birth Air Trainer, Nike's first cross-training shoe, and the Pegasus, one of Nike's best-selling running shoes of all time. Setting a design agenda for Nike is second nature for him. The challenge for Nike is making that fit into the financial rubric of a mature multinational giant.

It hasn't always succeeded. In 2004, Nike cofounder Phil Knight decided to step away from the company, handing over the reigns to William Perez, an analytic executive who came from the professionally managed if somewhat unexciting consumer chemical products company S. C. Johnson & Son, which makes products like Glade air freshener and Drano.

Historically, outsiders have had a tough time assimilating into Nike's culture, particularly at senior management levels. And Perez was no different. His attempts to elevate operational goals clashed with the company's creative talent. That's one reason why Knight forced Perez aside after just thirteen months on the job. Parker replaced him. "When Mark was elevated to the CEO role, it sent a message to the design community," says Sandy Bodecker, Nike's vice president of global design and a longtime friend and confidant of Parker.

41

Operation excellence remains important, but it isn't going to take a backseat to design.

Indeed, Parker makes sure design is at the core of everything Nike does these days. As we chat, the dirty-blond-haired Parker, who sports a mustache and beard, reaches for a booklet on the coffee table between us. It's a collection of eleven maxims handed out to all Nike employees the day they start working for the company. He puts on his reading glasses. "'Be a sponge,'" Parker reads, going into a monologue of design epiphanies. "'Curiosity is life. Assumption is death.'" He continues on for a while with more of the same. But what's curious is how much of it has nothing to do with performance. "'Technology, history, diversity, geography—today is a time of unparalleled interplay among cultures. Courageous new combinations of sports, fashion, music, movies, food, and the rest are redefining what is possible and relevant.'" You see, Parker, who was a top-notch runner in his college days, has kept Nike relevant by looking beyond sports for inspiration. No wonder he works in a museum.

In its earliest days, Nike didn't really care that much about fashion, music, movies, or food. It got its start in 1964 doing one thing really well—making the best running shoes available to hard-core runners who couldn't afford the dominant brand of the day, Adidas. The idea came to Knight, once a talented middle-distance runner at the University of Oregon in the late 1950s, when he was working toward his master's degree in business administration at Stanford University. He titled his thesis, penned in 1962, "Can Japanese sports shoes do to German sports shoes what Japanese cameras did to German cameras?" He argued that a low-priced running shoe from a Japanese company could challenge Adidas's monopoly of the U.S. market.

The idea stuck with him, even after graduating and taking a job at an accounting firm in Portland, Oregon. On a visit to Kobe, Japan, Knight dropped by the Onitsuka company unannounced, offering to distribute its Tiger running shoes in the United States. Onitsuka bit, and upon his return to Portland, Knight met with his college track coach, Bill Bowerman, hoping to sell him some shoes. Impressed with the idea, Bowerman offered to become a partner instead, and they formed Blue Ribbon Sports, as the company was known back then. The duo each invested five hundred dollars to order three hundred pairs of Tigers, which Knight sold from the back of his green Plymouth Valiant at high school track meets.

Knight took care of business, and Bowerman became the company's first designer. A legendary track coach who led Oregon to four NCAA titles and also coached the 1972 U.S. Olympic Track and Field squad, Bowerman was the archetypal coach, demanding excellence and withholding praise. In his biography, *Bowerman and the Men of Oregon: The Story of Oregon's Legendary Coach and Nike's Cofounder*, Olympic marathoner Kenny Moore writes of his roommate's assessment of their coach, "He speaks to us as does God. Intermittently." But Bowerman got the absolute best out of his athletes, many of whom came to love the man as a father figure. He was also an inveterate tinkerer, pioneering new training methods for runners and new materials for track surfaces. For years, he redesigned running shoes to see if he could make them lighter, figuring that over the course of a mile, even a few ounces adds up with each stride.

Within a few years, Bowerman came up with a shoe—the Cortez. He sent the shoe and design specifications to Onitsuka to manufacture them. It used nylon, where previous shoes used leather. It had a cushioning in the sole unlike any shoes before it. And it sold well to the track athletes who were becoming Blue Ribbon regulars, which convinced Knight and Bowerman to design more shoes, and to end their increasingly fragile relationship with Onitsuka.

The company needed a name for its shoes, and a logo so runners could identify them. Blue Ribbon's first employee, a runner Knight met at Stanford named Jeff Johnson, came up with the name—Nike, after the Greek goddess of victory. (It wasn't until 1978 that the company itself became known

Tiger Cortez, 1971. *(Courtesy of Nike, Inc.)*

as Nike.) And Carolyn Davidson, a graphic design student at Portland State University, came up with something of a rounded checkmark for a logo, earning thirty-five dollars for her work. These days, most of the world simply knows it as the Swoosh.

Back then, Nike was a runner's running shoe company, and no one embodied that more than Bowerman. He continued to coach many of the best runners in the United States. In 1967, he co-authored one of the earliest best sellers on the recreational running phenomenon, *Jogging: A Physical Fitness Program for All Ages*. He constantly designed and redesigned shoes, trying to simultaneously make them lighter yet more cushioned.

His biggest design breakthrough came at the breakfast table, and it's the stuff of legend at Nike, so much so that there are multiple versions of the story. Here's Nike's take on it, though you can find slight variations in Donald Katz's wonderful history of Nike, *Just Do It: The Nike Spirit in the Corporate World*, and Kenny Moore's biography of his coach.

Back in 1971, the University of Oregon resurfaced its track at Hayward Field with urethane, a hard surface that didn't lend itself to spikes. But flat-bottomed sneakers didn't provide enough friction for runners to maximize their speed. Bowerman needed a sole with texture, something that could both grip the track and provide cushioning when runners landed on it. At the kitchen table, Bowerman caught a glimpse of his waffle iron, and the idea hit him: Rather than landing hard on the solid sole, what if runners had their strides cushioned by an array of rubber studs, just like the metal prongs on a waffle iron?

Bowerman proceeded to stuff his waffle iron full of mold

45

clay. But he forgot to grease the waffle iron, so when it set, he couldn't pry the mold out. He ran out and bought a half-dozen or so more waffle irons, only to realize that he wanted a sole with waffle studs on it, not the inverse, which is what the waffle irons produced. Regardless, he had his solution.

Nike's first waffle-soled shoes were nothing short of spectacular. Runners raved about how comfortable they were, far beyond any jogging shoes previously made. And the shoes, like so many Nikes that came later, made a statement. They came in bright blue with a flashy yellow swoosh on the sides. Joggers loved them too, and Nike's sales exploded.

Even today, as Nike finds itself as much in the fashion business as the athletic one, there's still plenty of homage to Bowerman. The man died in 1999, but Parker works hard to make sure that his name is more than just a street that runs through the Nike campus. The last of those eleven maxims that Parker passes out to employees is "Remember the Man," a nod to the coach who is described as "strategically eccentric" and "tireless in his pursuit of innovation."

And yet Nike is a very different company from the one Bowerman and Knight founded. Performance remains paramount, but it's hardly Nike's only focus. One of Nike's most significant design breakthroughs has been its ability to bake hero worship into its shoe design. The company is often criticized for celebrating showmanship and extraordinary wealth, reflecting ugly aspects of American culture. The top brass, though, embraces the company's role in turning athletes into cultural icons. Nike chooses to see those stars as role models for the athletic potential in anyone who laces up sneakers, whether to swing a tennis racket or throw a football. That

46

hero worship, indeed, the entire Nike brand—is aspirational. "There's an innate desire to realize your own potential," Parker says.

There may be no one better at fueling those aspirations than Tinker Hatfield, Nike's vice president of creative design and the creator of seventeen models of Air Jordan shoes. Hatfield is as charming as he is creative. When we meet, he's wearing a white, patterned button-down shirt, untucked over well-worn blue jeans. He's sporting kicks that any self-respecting sneakerhead (industry vernacular for a rabid sport-shoe collector) would die for—a pair of limited-edition HTM Presto Boots, a design collaboration among Japanese disc-jockey-turned-designer Hiroshi Fujiwara, Hatfield, and Parker. The initials come from their first names.

Hatfield is the prototypical Nike employee. "Many of us have had a passion for sports long before we came here," Hatfield says. His was stronger than most. As a high schooler in the early 1970s, Hatfield was an all-American track star, specializing in hurdles and vaulting, and an all-state running back on the Central Linn High School football team in Oregon. He attended the University of Oregon, and was one of several early Nike employees who were coached by Bowerman. But an injury cut his track career short, forcing Hatfield to shift his drive toward his studies in architecture.

Hatfield joined Nike in 1981 to design offices and retail outlets. But four years into the job, he started designing shoes, and four years after that, he became creative director of product design. Over more than a quarter century, Hatfield has designed many of Nike's most iconic shoes. He was part of the group with Parker that came up with the Air Trainer.

47

He designed Nike's Air Max running shoes and its Air Huarache skeletal-shoe series. He's created tennis sneakers worn by Andre Agassi, Pete Sampras, and Roger Federer, and the basketball shoes sported by LeBron James and Kobe Bryant.

Hatfield, though, will forever be best known for his Air Jordan designs. He didn't design the first Air Jordans, the ones that earned NBA legend Michael Jordan a five-thousand-dollar fine each time he wore them during a game because the color scheme violated the league's uniform rules. But Hatfield, who designed the Air Jordan III and most of the twenty subsequent versions, redefined sport-shoe design with his approach to each new sneaker. Jordan's shoes have all the technical product advances that basketball players would expect from a high-end shoe. But what's made the Air Jordans different is that each new version has a story designed into it—one that Nike markets extraordinarily well.

Take the Air Jordan XIII, which Nike debuted in 1998. The shoe remains a favorite among sneakerheads, and retro releases of it continue to sell well. Hatfield's inspiration for the shoe came from watching Jordan on the court without the ball. "He'd float around the edges of the game, playing hard but being strategic about the next move," Hatfield recalls. "Then, he'd leap and do something spectacular." Just like a predatory cat, Hatfield thought. And when he saw a picture of a panther, the cat's eyes reminded him of Jordan's stare.

Hatfield started sketching a shoe with a pawlike sole. Black leather with ticking on the side that looked like fur. And an eye—a plastic orb—just above the outside ankle of each shoe that featured a hologram of the Jordan "Jumpman" logo.

When Hatfield presented the idea to Jordan during a break at a Los Angeles commercial shoot, he recalls Jordan being dumbstruck. "He looked at me and said, 'How did you know?'" Hatfield recalls. "Only my closest friends call me 'the Black Cat.'" Hatfield didn't know. "It was the first time he told me about being strategic and conserving his energy," Hatfield says. And it became the story that Nike used to sell the shoe.

That storytelling remains central to many of Hatfield's designs. His shoes don't merely protect feet from broken glass, or even improve athletic performance. They're canvases

49

he uses to tell stories that customers line up to buy. When Hatfield worked as an architect, he'd interview clients, asking not just the number of rooms they'd want but also about their lifestyle. He'd use that information to design a house that those clients might not have dreamed up on their own, but one that met their needs better than they could have imagined. For the Air Jordan 20s, Hatfield spent four days with Jordan at his house, interviewing him about his life, shooting hoops, and even digging through his closet to come up with a storyline. "It's added a different component to footwear design that isn't about performance," Hatfield says.

That may sound like marketing drivel, but the key to Nike's success is the understanding that its sneaker design isn't just about nailing the performance aspect. That only gets it in the game. Nike has perfected the art of getting its customers passionate about its products.

Like me. I'm a decent athlete, but I'm not much of a runner. I'll go for a two- or three-mile run when brutal weather prevents me from taking my bike out for spin. So on a particularly cold and rainy day, I put on my Nike Zoom Vomero+ shoes and head over to Seattle's Green Lake Park for a three-mile run. Days earlier, I had slipped a little sensor into the Vomero's sole, which connects to a receiver attached to my iPod. It's called Nike+, a twenty-nine-dollar contraption conjured up by Nike and Apple that lets me keep track of my speed, distance, and calories burned. And it's one of Nike's most innovative design breakthroughs.

50

As I head off, I tune into "We Don't Stop" by Michael Franti and Spearhead, an upbeat tune that's always been a pretty good performance enhancer for me. Then, a little less than a mile into my run, I press a button on my iPod. The music quiets down and a voice tells me that my pace is a 7-minute-38-second mile. That's about where I want it, I think. About a mile farther along, I press the iPod button again and find that I've slowed to an 8-minute mile. That's all the incentive I need. Within a hundred yards, my pace quickens to my earlier speed.

Sure, there are a handful of gadgets that help runners keep tabs on their performance. But they often feel like a chore to use. Even Nike's original training devices were the domain of the truly hard core. Nike+ opened the door to recreational runners with a simple observation: Between

Fits in your Nike+ shoe   Plugs into your iPod nano

NIKE + iPod

Nike+ sensor and receiver. *(Courtesy of Nike, Inc.)*

60 percent and 70 percent of people who run listen to music. It's hardly a revelation, but once Nike connected the music with performance, it created a new market by addressing a need runners had, even if they never knew they had it.

More than just tracking how far and fast runners go, Nike+ is helping the company build enduring relationships with them. When runners dock their iPods to their PCs, the software sucks up their run data—distance, pace, and calories burned. They have the tools online to graph their performance. Just like that virtual nudge I got running around Green Lake, the Web site gooses runners to speed up and log more miles simply by giving them data, because no one likes to see their performance numbers slip.

That's nifty enough. But Nike, with the help of New York advertising agency R/GA, created a virtual locker room with nikeplus.com. Dive deep into the service, as many of the customers have, and you'll find forums where runners meet and push one another to run farther and faster. On New Year's Day, 2010, for example, one Nike+ member used the tools on the site to create a competition among collegiate runners across the country to see which school would log the most mileage in the spring semester. There's a mapping feature where members post their favorite runs, making it easy for travelers, for instance, to pick out a route the next time they're visiting anywhere from Austin to Zurich. There are even coaching tips that give runners, for example, a twenty-eight-week running program to follow to prep them for their first marathon. "It moved us into a space where we were designing an experience," says Stefan Olander, global director of Nike consumer connections, who spearheaded the Nike+ effort.

52

Nike has used design to become a service company in the running shoe business. And it's been an amazing success. By the beginning of 2010, more than 2 million runners have logged more than 190 million miles on nikeplus.com. But at twenty-nine dollars a pop, the gadget, even though it sells in the millions, isn't much more than a rounding error for a $19-billion-a-year company. The real breakthrough is that Nike+ helped reverse the slide in the company's shrinking running shoe business. Over the years, companies that specialize in running shoes had steadily chipped away at Nike's once dominant share, knocking it down to 48 percent in the United States, before Nike+ was launched, according to Sports-OneSource, a market research firm. Just two years later, Nike trainers accounted for 61 percent of the market.

Stop and think about the significance of that for a second. Nike didn't turn its fortunes around with a high-profile ad campaign or a massive rebranding effort. It revived its business with a little sensor in a shoe and social networking, one of the most important cultural artifacts of the day. Nike didn't create a social network simply because it felt pressure to join the Web 2.0 world. It created Nike+ because it figured out that the service filled an unmet need that runners had. It came up with a product that generated data for which many runners yearn, and it coupled that with a community where they found an emotional connection. "If we do this well, we can have a relationship that's sustainable," says Nike's Olander.

Nike continues to experiment with technology and push into new markets. "Nike's culture, at its best, is the best of sports, the best of what makes athletes great," Parker says. Hypercompetitive, driven, team-focused. "There's a very strong analogy there." Maybe the most important quality from a design standpoint is that great athletes aren't averse to risk. They want to be the guy who gets the basketball outside the three-point line, down by two with just a few seconds on the clock. "We love taking risks. We don't mind when we pursue something and it doesn't pan out," Parker says. "You learn something, you move on, and you make something better the next time you go at it." Remember that. You'll read about companies later in the book willing to embrace failure. It's something great design companies have in common.

When Nike first took a run at the skateboard business, it fell flat on its face. And it's a great example of how Nike's formidable marketing skills can carry the company only so far. Back in 1997, the company produced a series of clever ads leading up to the Summer X Games to demonstrate its kinship with skate culture. One starts with a flashlight-wielding policeman breaking up a doubles tennis match between two middle-aged couples. There is a sign on the wall behind the court that reads NO TENNIS and another hanging on the net that says TENNIS PROHIBITED. As the officer steps closer and harasses the players, one couple makes a break, scaling the chain-link fence next to the court. And then the tagline comes: "What if we treated all athletes the way we treat skateboarders?"

Great ad, but that's pretty much all Nike had to offer. "The skate community loved it, but we had nothing to back it up," says global design vice president Bodecker, who led the skateboarding effort. Nike's basketball shoes, mostly the

Blazer, Dunk, and Air Jordan models, were widely used by skateboarders already. So the company didn't really put a lot of effort into designing skateboard-specific models. "We had a history, but we didn't have a commitment," Bodecker says. "We didn't really cut it from the product side."

The operations side was equally derelict. Nike didn't create a sales force to specifically sell shoes to skate shops, but instead counted on its existing account reps to forge new relationships in a business that was entirely foreign to them. And as good as the ads were, it had no real grassroots marketing, such as sponsoring events and getting involved with the sport at local levels. It wasn't part of the culture. "We weren't perceived as giving back on a regular basis," Bodecker says. "When Nike is successful, we commit one hundred percent. We didn't do that." Contrast that to a company such as Vans, which has been part of the fabric of skateboarding since it first sold shoes in 1966. It doesn't just sell skate shoes; the company has built skate parks in California and Florida. It sponsors bands favored by skate punks, such as Slayer, The Hives, and Guttermouth. And it sponsors competitions, such as Vans Downtown Showdown, where top skateboarding pros vie for cash prizes.

Just a look around Bodecker's office suggests how deep into skateboard culture Nike dived. Like Parker's, it's overflowing with curios and gewgaws collected over time. He's got Asian nesting dolls on his windowsill and a Hulk action figure next to his computer monitor. Just behind his desk, there's a collection of five bass guitars. And behind a conference table, there's a huge painting, a collage of pastel-colored cartoon hands, the kind with only three fingers and a thumb,

55

by KAWS, a pop-culture artist who has designed limited-edition sneakers for Nike.

But the most telling curios among Bodecker's collection are the skateboard decks, more than a dozen, stacked up along the wall as you enter the office. The most prominent: three boards made by Consolidated Skateboards, a favorite among the tattooed and pierced skateboard crowd. It's a company that's spent considerable brainpower railing against corporate behemoth Nike's entry into the skate business. One of the screens that rotates through the home page on its Web site mocks Nike with the phrase "Don't Do It," and it exhorts customers to support local skateboard shops "even if they carry those faggot shoes some people seem to like."

Consolidated took its displeasure at Nike so far as to design its "Corporate Kiss Ass" series—the three decks that now sit in Bodecker's office. The graphics on the bottom of one board focus on Phil Knight sporting a blingy gold chain with a dollar sign dangling from it and wearing a baseball cap with its brim off to the side. The second has eyebrow-pierced Parker in a sleeveless muscle shirt, showing off a tattoo, with his limousine idling in the background. And the last features Bodecker, wearing a T-shirt that reads "The Exploiter" in front of a sales projection chart with revenue soaring skyward. There's a substance, decidedly brown, covering the tip of his nose, presumably the inspiration for the name of the series of decks. Consolidated never wound up producing more than those three decks, which Bodecker bought through an intermediary when they were auctioned. He smiles at the subterfuge. And he's amused by the suggestion that big corporate Nike couldn't be authentic enough to be successful in the skateboard business.

56

Nike SB is now the top-selling brand in skateboard shops, and it got there by focusing on design. Rather than merely rebranding basketball shoes, the company sat down with skateboarders to understand the shortcomings of existing shoes. "We made sure we hired people who were of the culture," Bodecker says. And rather than just pushing its shoes on skateboarders, Nike listened. Heel bruising is a problem for some, so Nike designers tinkered, tweaking the Zoom Air insole, initially created for running, walking, and training shoes. Boards sometimes land hard on top of skateboarders' feet during tricks, so Nike beefed up the padding in the shoe's tongue.

With a quality product, the company set its marketing forces loose, this time hiring Paul Rodriguez, an X Games gold medalist, to endorse its shoes. P-Rod, like most top Nike athletes, didn't just affix his name to the shoes. He participated in the process. He gave the company pointers, then tested prototypes—more than a dozen different sock liners, for example—at the skate park at his Southern California home and at Nike's indoor skate facility in Portland, Oregon. "Paul is really good about describing little nuances that, for him, are very important," Bodecker says. Rodriguez pushed Nike to modify the grip on the shoe's outsole so that it was just sticky enough to help flick his board to do certain tricks.

It didn't hurt, either, that Rodriguez gave Nike credibility. His P-Rod line remains a favorite among hard-core skateboarders as well as fashionistas sporting the street-punk look. Nike also poached staff from established skate companies, people who helped teach Nike the industry. And it dived

57

Nike SB Zoom Air P-Rod III. *(Courtesy of Nike, Inc.)*

deep into giving back to the community, sponsoring skate events and producing skate videos. "When we did make the commitment to connect to that consumer, to be a part of that culture, to take those insights and turn them into innovation, it resonated," Parker says. "It's been incredibly successful."

It says much about the transformation Nike has made over the years. Sports excellence is clearly at the core of the company culture. Nike World Headquarters is a place where sport is worshipped. All Nike employees toil in buildings named after athletes who have worn the company's shoes, icons such as Ken Griffey Jr., Pete Sampras, and Michael Jordan. When I interview Parker, it's in his office atop the John McEnroe building. Workers can attend meetings in the Tiger Woods Conference Center, work out in the Lance Armstrong gym, and grab a bite to eat in the cafeteria in the Mia Hamm building. There are busts of lesser-known athletes sprinkled around the campus.

But Nike has come to realize that as important as athletes

58

are to its business, basketball and skateboard shoes are just as much about fashion as they are about performance. Maybe even more so. So the company has turned to KAWS, as well as to Los Angeles tattoo artist Mr. Cartoon and Japanese artist Katsuya Terada, among others, to stay hip. It's not alone. Rhode Island School of Design president John Maeda designed Reebok's limited-edition Ventilator Timetanium shoe in 2007. Adidas has turned to fashion designer Jeremy Scott, who has created dresses for the rock star Björk, to come up with its JS Wings shoe, a limited-edition high-top with angel wings flapping off to the sides. The late British designer Alexander McQueen conjured up Puma's Ribcage line, designed with brightly colored veins and tendons, inspired by human anatomy.

Like the others, Nike builds cachet by rationing its high-design shoes, and even putting serial numbers on them. It's not unusual to find the most fanatic of fans pitching tents outside Niketown stores, camping overnight to get their hands on a rare pair of kicks. As those shoes become ever more coveted, Nike parcels a handful out to such tony shops as the Paris fashion boutique Colette and New York City's Dave's Quality Meat.

It would be easy to dismiss this success as great marketing. And there's no question that Nike is among the best at the game. Years ago, it set a standard—with ads such as Spike Lee's commercials featuring himself as Mars Blackmon idolizing Michael Jordan, or the company's "Bo Knows" ads, with multisport talent Bo Jackson playing unlikely sports such as tennis and hockey. It's a standard that even it sometimes has

59

a hard time reaching. And the thirty-five-dollar Swoosh may be the most potent branding symbol ever.

Parker doesn't dismiss the power of marketing. But he's a designer, and he believes that all the marketing in the world couldn't sell a lousy product. "The most powerful marketing tool is the product itself," Parker says.

3

LEGO

Paal Smith-Meyer is waving a *BusinessWeek* article in front of me about LEGO's resurgence. "The Brick Is Back," reads the headline, and Smith-Meyer, who runs LEGO's New Business Group, is reveling in the positive press, particularly happy to share the story from the magazine for which I wrote for nearly a decade. LEGO, which struggled mightily in the early to mid-2000s, leaned heavily on design to turn its financial fortunes around. In the article, LEGO executive vice president of markets and products Mads Nipper says, "With our arrogance, we thought being LEGO allowed us to do anything." Great quote, I think.

But here's the odd thing: In all my days working for *BusinessWeek,* I can't for the life of me recall an article in the magazine about the revival of the Danish toy company. I'm a pretty avid *BusinessWeek* reader, and I'm certain I'd remember a piece, particularly one with juicy, self-effacing quotes from senior executives, like this one.

As I look more closely, something seems off. The article is written by Patrick S. Mitchell. I know most of the writers at the magazine, and there's never been a journalist on the staff with that name. At least no one I can recall. A freelancer? The layout doesn't look quite right, either. The color of the border at the top of the page is pretty close. But there aren't any of the creative touches that my former colleagues in the graphics department use to make articles more navigable.

And then I catch it. The issue date of the magazine is March 22/29, 2010. That's more than a year into the future. I look up at Smith-Meyer, who just smiles. Turns out he wrote the piece himself in 2005 and used a graphics program to mimic *BusinessWeek*'s layout. He distributed it to LEGO's senior managers back then to tell the story of LEGO's turnaround—before it happened. He wanted to give the company's leaders a road map, albeit one that describes the route from the rearview mirror. And that byline? Smith-Meyer came up with what he thought was a *BusinessWeek*-y name, instead of his Norwegian one, using his initials.

It's mid-January and we're sitting in a conference room in one of the dozen LEGO buildings that dot Billund, a sleepy town in a remote part of western Denmark that would be even sleepier if not for LEGO. From the moment you land in Billund's efficient airport, LEGO is nearly inescapable. Huge LEGO bricks—five hundred times the size of the toy versions—mark the various company-owned buildings around town. A gigantic "minifigure" (known as a "minifig" to LEGO fans), one of those iconic people that populate LEGO towns and drive LEGO cars, greets visitors heading toward LEGOLAND. That's the amusement park the

64

company opened in 1968, just as its construction toys were reaching into the farthest corners of the earth.

The colors inside LEGO offices are the fire-engine red, canary yellow, and Kelly green of the bricks packed inside every box. And those bricks are everywhere, in case a worker or visitor has a hankering to build: on tables in conference rooms, at reception desks. Nearly every office, it seems, is decorated with elaborate LEGO creations. There's a life-size Harry Potter riding his Nimbus 2000 broomstick, and a giraffe with its neck reaching toward the ceiling. Winnie the Pooh, Piglet, Eeyore, and Tigger sit nearby, made from hundreds of building blocks by the twenty-four in-house designers who work exclusively creating plastic masterpieces for the company.

Smith-Meyer is something of a minstrel in this playland, a worker who brings a sense of wonder to a place he's constantly trying to reinvent. Instead of handing out business cards, LEGO executives pass out minifigs in their likeness with their name, e-mail, and phone number printed on the chest and back. Smith-Meyer notes that his minifig has a full head of hair only because LEGO doesn't make them with the receding hairline that has come a bit early for the thirty-six-year-old. The soul patch on Smith-Meyer's chin and his long sideburns are re-created as a full mustache and beard on his minifig. His black shirt rests untucked over his blue jeans.

Smith-Meyer describes himself as an "innovation nomad." He earned a degree in product design in 1999 from Northumbria University, the alma mater of today's most famous industrial designer, Apple's Jonathan Ive. Smith-Meyer joined LEGO a year later, working on its Racers and Creator

65

models before moving through other product divisions and, finally, landing his current gig looking for new opportunities for the company.

Within a few years of Smith-Meyer's arrival, though, LEGO was struggling to keep its existing business afloat. The company strayed from its strength in construction toys, following others into such unfamiliar businesses as action figures and apparel. It decided to expand its theme-park business beyond Billund, adding vacation spots in Windsor, England; Günzburg, Germany; and Carlsbad, California.

In its thirst for growth, it took design for granted. Its construction toy business withered, a victim of management neglect. That quote from Nipper about LEGO's arrogance—he might not have actually said it, but there's little doubt of its veracity. LEGO thought it could do anything when in fact it was struggling to succeed at the one thing in which it once excelled. As a result, the company's sales fell off a cliff, dropping by nearly a third from 2002 to 2004. It lost more than $500 million in that period, leading to company layoffs.

But by the end of the decade, the brick really was back. LEGO refocused its business and returned to designing great toys. It sold off a controlling interest in its theme parks and found licensing partners to make LEGO-branded clothes and video games. And it went back to building its brick business.

In just a few short years, the company became a financial pillar, one of the strongest toy companies on the face of the planet. In 2008, in the midst of the worst recession in decades, LEGO's sales and profits climbed, both solidly in double digits.

Design made it happen.

Like many great design companies, LEGO was born from a craftsman's hands. In 1932, carpenter Ole Kirk Kristiansen struggled to make ends meet. His business, making doors, windows, and cupboards for the farmers in his district, was hit hard by the global depression. Worse still, his wife died that year, leaving him to raise their four children.

To make ends meet, Kristiansen turned to toys, hand-crafted wooden ones, figuring that the one area where families wouldn't cut back so drastically was gifts for their children. He went from village to village, selling such playthings as carved ducks with wheels on the bottom and strings attached to the necks that could be dragged across the floor, trucks, and airplanes.

The company didn't flourish initially, though it sustained Kristiansen, a second wife, and their family through the Depression. As it grew, Kristiansen realized he needed a name for the company, and settled on LEGO, a shortening of the Danish phrase *leg godt,* which means "play well." Years later, after LEGO began producing construction toys, Kristiansen learned that the word *lego* is Latin for "I assemble."

It wasn't until after World War II that LEGO evolved into a construction toy company. Back then, high-quality wood was increasingly hard to find. At the same time, a new material emerged that threatened wood workers but also offered great potential for all kinds of manufacturing indus-tries, including toy making: plastic.

67

Rather than shun the new material, as some of his LEGO colleagues suggested he should, Kristiansen embraced it.

When LEGO bought a plastic injection molding machine in 1947, it was the first Danish toy company to do so. Two years later, LEGO produced the first "binding blocks," predecessors of the iconic bricks of today.

Truth be told, the original blocks didn't really bind all that well. They were square and rectangle bits of plastic with studs on the top. They had slits on the sides to attach windows and doors. But there wasn't any design feature that allowed one block to snap snugly with another. When kids built structures more than a few bricks high, they became unstable, crumbling down with the barest of nudges. LEGO didn't have a huge engineering department back then, so it took the company nearly a decade to solve the problem. In 1957, they figured it out, designing bricks that had interior tubes, flush with the bottom of the brick, that solidly latched onto the studs on the top of another brick.

So if you ask executives at LEGO, still owned by the Kristiansen family, to point to the most important date in the company's history, it wouldn't be that day in 1947 when "Ole Kirk," as he's known in the corridors of LEGO, bought the injection molding machine, or even the day they started to make those early construction bricks. No, the day they would point to—and they'd even give you the precise minute—is January 28, 1958, at 1:58 in the afternoon. At that moment, Ole Kirk's son, Godtfred, submitted the application to the Danish Patent and Trademark Office in Copenhagen to patent the LEGO building brick system.

68   There are few toys in the world as iconic as a rectangular LEGO brick with two rows of four studs each. You can probably picture it now—fire-engine red, right? But it would

LEGO brick.
(© 2010 The Lego Group)

be wrong to peg the brilliance of LEGO on just the brick. LEGO has flourished because it created a system for building. The patent didn't merely protect the brick design. It covered the method by which those bricks snap together. That system, which lets kids create cars, ships, and buildings with the same fundamental pieces, is the core of LEGO's franchise.

In its darkest days, that's what LEGO forgot.

The company's problems began in the late 1990s, when it stopped focusing on design. Back then, company executives wanted to extend the brand, venturing off on wild forays into new product development. The prototypical example: Galidor, a legendary bomb inside the walls of LEGO. The Galidor line, launched in 2002, was all about action figures, like the hero Nick Bluetooth. The figures could barely be taken apart and reassembled—arms, for example, could be interchanged. But the figures were little different from toys offered by scores of other manufacturers. They didn't require building skills or much in the way of imagination, the hallmark of the more traditional LEGO construction toys.

Worse still, LEGO branched into a whole new business about which it knew little. The company coproduced a kids' TV show called *Galidor: Defenders of the Outer Dimension*. The story line was meant to add detail to the action figures, giving kids more reason to buy them. But the shows sparked

Galidor's Nick Bluetooth character.
(© 2010 The Lego Group)

little interest. It was a Saturday morning cartoon cliché, a predictable action adventure story that was easily dismissed as a thirty-minute advertisement for the toy line. The show, which ran in the United States on the Fox network, lasted two seasons. When it went off the air, sales of the action figures faded.

Even within its core construction toy business, LEGO was foundering. LEGO managers had given designers free rein to come up with ever more imaginative new creations. And they took it. Left to their own devices, designers conjured up increasingly complex models, many of which required the company to make new components—the various bricks, doors, helmets, and heads that come in a rainbow of colors and fill every LEGO box. By 2004, the number of components had exploded, climbing from about 7,000 to 12,400 in just seven years. Of course, supply costs went through the roof too.

But even more troubling was that the new designs weren't resonating with kids. That freedom to create elaborate new designs had a price. "It was making us more stupid," Smith-Meyer says. All you needed to do was look at the fire truck in its LEGO City line. It went from being a conventional hook-and-ladder rig to a futuristic hot rod. Its cockpit-like pod for a driver was nearly twice the size of the back of the truck, where presumably all the firefighting gear was stored.

The truck looked cool to the adult designers, but kids hated it. "It totally failed," says Nipper, the executive vice president. The design free-for-all turned the LEGO City line, once among the largest pieces of LEGO's business, into a shell of its former self, accounting for just 3 percent of the company's total revenue, down from roughly 13 percent in 1999. "It literally almost evaporated," Nipper says.

Looking back, Nipper doesn't find fault with the designers. "Management was to blame," Nipper says. "The same people who were doing crappy products then are making world-class products today." Managers, rather, let those designers go wild. And, Smith-Meyer says, they did. "We almost did innovation suicide. We didn't do a lot of clever components. We did a lot of stylized pieces," Smith-Meyer says. "We wanted to be Philippe Starck"—the French industrial, interior, and furniture designer famous for everything from juicers to motorcycles. LEGO had assumed it would flourish by giving its designers whatever pieces they asked for in order to unleash their creativity. Instead, costs soared as the models veered toward the esoteric. Design, a hallmark of Danish culture, had run amok. The company's problems—Galidor, overly stylized models, its financial slide—all came to a head. The business that began in earnest with that patent application nearly fifty years earlier was in jeopardy.

Just as design pushed LEGO to the precipice, it helped bring the company back. But here's the paradox: Instead of giving designers free rein to conjure up their most brilliant creations to save the company, LEGO tied their hands. Instead of rubber-stamping nearly every request for a new component, LEGO put each one to a vote among designers. Only the top vote getters—the ones that other designers imagined they could use—would be added to the palette. And it eliminated rarely used pieces, slashing the total number of components to about 7,000, the same number as in 1997.

LEGO also forced designers to come out of their cocoons

72

and work with noncreative staff. At the earliest stages of product development, marketing managers, who had detailed research on the types of products kids wanted, helped guide development. Manufacturing personnel weighed in on production costs before a prototype ever saw the light of day. Gone were the days when designers could go wherever their imaginations took them.

Let's step back for a second and think back to Porsche's design model. The carmaker never brings its product ideas to committee. From its first days, Ferry Porsche decreed that the only folks who knew how to make a Porsche were those employed inside the company's walls. So how can LEGO succeed by being different? Just as Apple doesn't have the sole key to design success, neither does Porsche nor, for that matter, LEGO. And that's really the point. Much as business gurus might try to gin up a one-size-fits-all strategy, there isn't one. LEGO couldn't succeed by mimicking Porsche's strategy because the people who design its cars are the core audience. As much as they might speculate, the LEGO designers don't really know what seven-year-old boys want. So LEGO took some control away from its designers.

It was particularly challenging because design is LEGO's key competitive advantage. Over the years, various rivals have emerged, making bricks that snap together with LEGO blocks at a fraction of the cost. Montreal-based MEGA Brands is the current thorn in LEGO's side. Companies such as Tyco Toys came before it with a similar strategy. But kids and their parents keep buying LEGO, and not simply because of their belief that the quality is better. They buy LEGO because the company offers the most creative collection of models, not

LEGO City firetruck, 2001. *(© 2010 The Lego Group)*

merely a collection of bricks. Confining designers ran the risk of diminishing that competitive advantage.

Except it didn't. The changes started in 2004, gradually reshaping the product lines. In 2005, the futuristic LEGO City fire truck got an overhaul. Gone were the cockpit and the tiny rear section. It looked like a fire truck again. "A five-year-old doesn't need to be told who are the heroes," Nipper says. "He projects it onto [the toy]." Sales of the City line started perking up, leading LEGO to update the police and construction models too. By 2008, City reclaimed its spot at

74

LEGO City firetruck, 2005. *(© 2010 The Lego Group)*

the top of LEGO's portfolio, accounting for 20 percent of
the company's revenue. "It has refound its identity," Nipper
says.

It was an aha moment. It may sound counterintuitive,
but LEGO found that design, at least within its walls, thrives
with some constraints. That might send chills up the spines
of some in the design world. The idea of fencing in designers,
forcing them to play in a confined space, runs counter to the
notion that design needs to be set free. But the component
limits gave designers just enough direction to come up with

75

some of the company's most successful products to date. "If you put guiding principles in place, you empower people to make the right decision," Smith-Meyer says. And remember, he's a designer.

LEGO executives realized the company couldn't design products the way it once had, gambling on the ingenuity of its brightest creative lights. It needed to formalize the process, to make sure that the best ideas from designers actually aligned with what its consumers would want and what its supply chain could afford.

The company created the LEGO Innovation Model, a detailed methodology for product development. It's the most detailed design process of any company you'll read about in this book. "We wanted some kind of structure around the way we design products," says LEGO senior director Morten Juel Willemann, who helps managers navigate the process. It comes with snazzy brochures, handed out to LEGO staff, with flowcharts and schematics diagramming the process by which new models come to life. And it's full of acronyms, such as D4B (Design for Business) that spell out each stage of product development.

The formalized design process will be familiar to those who have studied design strategy. It has four discrete steps. The first phase—known as P0—is the stage where LEGO designers, marketers, finance staff, and others look broadly at potential business opportunities, study consumer trends, and come up with ideas for their business groups. P1 is the stage that the designers refer to as the ideation phase. It's when the product groups start brainstorming concepts that might address the opportunities outlined in the previous stage.

Then it's time to refine ideas. In P2, the best concepts from the previous phase are developed, business cases are prepared, and prototypes are created. In the final phase, P3, LEGO executives look at account development and manufacturing costs, and decide which products to take to market. The company flies in top executives from around the globe to help assess the products' prospects in each region and to establish marketing commitments. "The markets used to see the product and campaigns as a buffet," Willemann says. They'd pick and choose among the models they thought would do best in their region. But since LEGO sells the exact same toys in every market around the globe, that often meant that marketing commitments were a patchwork, strong in Europe for one model but virtually nonexistent in North America for another. "We make sure there is commitment early," Willemann says.

LEGO began rolling out the process in 2004, but it wasn't until 2007 that its entire product line was created under the new model. And that year's portfolio registered the lowest design cost in recent LEGO history, a 55 percent drop in the three years since the process began. What's more, product lead times were cut in half to twelve months. Most tellingly of all, though, is that sales increased 42 percent in four years, and Willemann believes much of the credit goes to the new process. "There is no doubt that it has been a contributing factor to a highly relevant retail portfolio," Willemann says.

Now that the business is humming, Willemann is encouraging managers to back off the process—if only a bit—to give

LEGO designers more room to test new ideas. "We need to say, 'It's okay to let your creativity loose. It's okay to be off-process,'" Willemann says. "We need to dial up the creativity, the nonstructured part, more."

One way it has started to do that is by looking for designs outside tiny Billund. As creative as LEGO's 120 designers are, executives knew there were thousands of other LEGO designers creating masterpieces: their customers. It was all right there on the Web, works of art by LEGO fans. The Taj Mahal. The Empire State Building. Airplanes. Cars. Entire cities. Creativity abounded. "The adult community was making amazing stuff without any new parts," Smith-Meyer says.

LEGO may be a kid's toy, but it has an intensely loyal following among adults. Folks like the ones who have come to the Oregon Convention Center in Portland on a damp, gray Friday two months after I chatted with Smith-Meyer. They're attending BrickFest 2009, an annual gathering of AFOLs. That's "Adult Fans of LEGO" to the uninitiated. More than two hundred of them come to show off MOCs, LEGO lingo for "My Own Creation." On one table is a bust of Kiss front man Ace Frehley. Just around the corner, there's a monochromatic mosaic of the Portland skyline with Mount Hood in the background. And, in a wonderful bit of self-referential work, there's a LEGO diorama of BrickFest itself. At the real show, vendors sell T-shirts, including one that reads "SNOT," which stands for "Studs Not On Top," a style of building in which LEGO pieces are used on their sides or upside down.

78

These folks don't just have their own language. There's an entire subculture of fanaticism that rivals anything a Star Trek convention can offer. Hard-core LEGO fans subscribe to magazines such as *BrickJournal,* a quarterly rundown of all things LEGO. They listen to podcasts with building tips on LAMLradio ("LEGO and More LEGO"). They check out The Brothers Brick blog for inspiration from some of the most intricate and ornate creations from around the world.

At BrickFest, fans attend seminars on everything from using software programs to create and save LEGO model instructions for rebuilding later, to SNOT building techniques. One of the most animated discussions comes during the "Sorting and Storing" panel, where AFOLs, who have hundreds of thousands of LEGO pieces, discuss and sometimes debate the best methods for keeping their bricks organized—pondering the merits of organizing by shape versus color. When the discussion turns to the best methods for transporting MOCs to shows such as BrickFest, a panelist mentions watching one builder stuff his creation in the back of an SUV without any protection. The man sitting across the aisle from me shivers and makes a *brrrrr* sort of noise, as though someone just ran fingernails across a chalkboard.

For years, LEGO watched adult fans from afar, amused by hard-core hobbyists but seemingly uninterested in engaging them. But in the early 2000s, a handful of LEGO executives realized that those fanatics could help the company revamp its design process. They could put into words the joys and frustrations of LEGO that seven-year-old fans can't.

LEGO first reached out to those adult customers while it was developing the follow-up to its blockbuster robotics

79

modeling kit, Mindstorms. Initially launched in 1998, Mindstorms was developed with the help of MIT mathematician and computer scientist Seymour Papert. The centerpiece of the toy is a 4.5-inch-by-3-inch brick with a processor inside that users can program with an attached computer. That brick sits at the core of an assemblage of LEGO pieces designed in whatever shape a customer wants. It reacts to input picked up by sensors, sending commands to motors that move the robot about.

Mindstorms actually came out of LEGO's education unit—the company originally thought it would be a niche product that could be used to help teach kids about robotics. But when it hit store shelves, adults, particularly those with computer-programming skills, voraciously gobbled it up. And they built amazing creations, from a tail-wagging dog to a blackjack-dealing machine. Kids liked it too—schools bought Mindstorms kits to teach robotics, and an organization called FIRST LEGO League sprouted, launching competitions among young people to build the best bot.

It was a phenomenon unlike anything LEGO had ever experienced. And yet the company, which had created a skunkworks unit to launch the original Mindstorms separate from the politics of the organization, knew it needed a different approach for the next version. As popular as Mindstorms was, its computer language was a bit too complex for kids. Better sensors would open up even more programming possibilities. But that stuff wasn't really LEGO's forte.

So Mindstorms boss and LEGO senior director Søren Lund broke from standard operating procedure. Adult fans of Mindstorms, and even some kids, used online forums to show off their latest creations and get tips to help hurdle design challenges. Lund reached out to a handful of the most creative Mindstorms users with a request: He wanted their help with designing Mindstorms NXT, the product's second iteration.

Lund knew it was a dicey proposition. There could be legal questions about the ownership of the development ideas. There could be leaks that would help competitors. But Lund's biggest fear was that getting lawyers involved would bog down the process. "We decided not to tell management," Lund says. "Sometimes it's better to ask for forgiveness."

Turns out that hard-core customers have a pretty good idea about what they want in a product. Some of their ideas were too complex to pull off or too niche to matter. But there were plenty—such as an ultrasonic sensor that measures distance and movement—that made their way into Mindstorms NXT because of the Mindstorms User Panel. And the cost: de minimis. The customers felt honored to be included in the process, and were happy to receive some LEGO models for their efforts. "You can have a dialogue with your customers as long as you tell them what you're going to do," Lund says.

Think back a chapter to the folks at Nike. Geeky LEGO fans may not seem to have much in common with world-class skateboarders such as Paul Rodriguez or a golf icon such as Tiger Woods, but they do. Just as Nike turned to those athletes to help shape its products, LEGO leaned on its fringe customers—the most extreme, hard-core users—to help it with design. Like Nike, LEGO realized that those customers understood the product so well that they'd come up with ideas that the masses would appreciate even if they didn't know to ask for them. Those customers helped the company

81

meet the most precious customer needs—those unstated, even unconsidered, desires. Companies able to deliver those inevitably have a hit on their hands.

With Mindstorms NXT, which hit shelves in 2006, customers created robots that could play music on a xylophone, solve a Rubik's Cube, or fill a dog bowl with kibble. It became LEGO's best-selling product of the year. And it was the company's second-best-selling product in 2007.

Another aha moment—turning a piece of design over to customers. This wasn't some glorified focus group that asks customers to give prospective models a thumbs-up or -down. LEGO figured out how to prosper by soliciting its most hard-core fans for ideas. And not only did it make Mindstorms better, it made those customers—an influential group among buyers—even more loyal.

Just as LEGO reached out to customers to help with design, it was losing its grip on the brick. That patent that Godt-fred Christiansen (who spelled his last name differently from his father) filed back in 1958 was withering under attack from MEGA Brands, which had won a series of legal battles giving it the right to make bricks compatible with LEGO pieces.

Rather than spending time and effort fighting those companies, LEGO has begun working with a few of the smaller ones that pose little threat, trying its hand at venture capital. It's providing seed money and guidance to entrepreneurs keen to start LEGO-related businesses. It started with Adam Reed Tucker, a Chicago architect who creates massive scale models of some of the world's best-known buildings from the plastic bricks. Tucker thought there might be a business selling smaller versions of his creations in souvenir shops, places where LEGO models aren't typically sold. He approached the company and found Smith-Meyer.

LEGO experimented. Tucker created a sixty-eight-piece model of the Sears Tower in Chicago, one that was relatively easy and not particularly time-consuming to put together. LEGO initially sent him enough bricks to build two thousand Sears Towers. Tucker sorted and stuffed them into packaging that LEGO also sent him, with a picture of the finished model. Perhaps most important, the packaging included the phrase "Published by the LEGO Group" on the side. It was a huge step for a company that's intensely protective of its brand to hand it over to a small-time entrepreneur. But in a few months, the gift shop in the Sears Tower (which changed its name in 2009 to the Willis Tower) sold every twenty-dollar box Tucker put together. That was enough to convince LEGO that there was a real business, selling not just models of that building but of iconic buildings all over the world. It created a new product line, LEGO Architecture, the company's first partnership with a member of its community, and launched models of the John Hancock Center in Chicago and New York's Empire State Building, among others.

The models from LEGO Architecture are a bit more refined than the original Sears Tower. The packaging is slicker and comes with a glossy booklet that includes details on the architecture, engineering, and construction of each building. While they don't sell in the same volume as other LEGO models, they've become among the fastest-moving items in souvenir shops. The store at Seattle's Space Needle, another LEGO Architecture model, sold three hundred kits in the first nine days on its shelves. "In the area of souvenir businesses,

Empire State Building
New York City, New York, USA

Ages
10+
21002

Cont. **77** pcs
Construction model

Landmark series
1st edition
designed by
Adam Reed Tucker

Booklet included
with details on
design and history

Building Toy

84

we're disruptive," Smith-Meyer says. What's more, the kits command much higher prices than traditional LEGOs. The LEGO City police car or LEGO Creator helicopter sells for about ten cents a brick. LEGO Architecture? Try thirty to forty cents a brick.

There aren't many toy companies in the world with more brand power than LEGO. Three generations of kids have built cars, cities, and spaceships with LEGO's iconic bricks. Its logo—the red square with the rounded white letters—is immediately identifiable to most of the developed world, and to a bunch of developing nations as well.

But like Nike's Parker, Nipper is sanguine about the power of the brand. It opens doors, getting kids and parents alike to consider LEGO products. But if those products don't engage them, kids will move very quickly to the next toy. "Children are ruthless in that they are very demanding about what they want to buy," Nipper says. "If your offer does not stack up, they will go somewhere else." Brand is important, but, as LEGO learned, design is crucial. "If LEGO is the Catholic Church, then design is the Sistine Chapel," Nipper says. "It is the holiest of the holy."

4

OXO

There's a smell coming from the kitchen at the lower Manhattan headquarters of OXO. The aroma is mouth-watering and decidedly identifiable. Brownies. Man, they smell good. But nobody's eating them. Amanda Luke, a senior product manager, has sunk a spatula into the pan as the brownies are cooling. It's just sitting there. Meanwhile, Evan Abel, a product engineer, slips a thermometer into the brownies. Turns out they're testing a prototype brownie spatula, designed specifically to slip under the brownie and scoop it out without leaving chunks behind. When the testing concludes, the brownies, prodded by thermometers and various spatulas, are set out for OXO's staff to devour.

At OXO, the renowned maker of design-centric kitchenware, the food seems to come nonstop. Earlier that day, a group of employees had gone through their twice-a-week "salad club" ritual. Five of the club's members step away from their desks at half past noon and start cleaning lettuce, slicing cucumbers, and dicing peppers, using OXO's salad spinner, mandoline slicer, and polypropylene cutting boards. At one o'clock, all twenty members descend upon the feast.

Some two hours later, three pies arrive in the kitchen—cherry, sour cream apple, and pecan. It's a birthday celebration, delivered with OXO's pie-serving utensils. Within a few minutes, only crumbs are left. "It's impossible to lose weight here," says the improbably slender Hideyo Hayami, the manager for OXO's Japanese operations. She takes another bite of her sour cream apple pie.

Just as Porsche employees love cars and Nike is populated with athletes, OXO is full of foodies. And as with those other firms, OXO began when its founder, Sam Farber, grew frustrated with existing products and decided to create something better. Unlike Ferry Porsche or Phil Knight, Farber wasn't a young entrepreneur just getting his start. He had already retired, a pioneer in the housewares business with his company, Copco, known widely for its brightly colored enamel teakettles.

Back in the late 1980s, Farber was vacationing in the south of France when he noticed his wife Betsey's mild arthritis causing pain while she peeled apples for a tart. The thin metal peeler was hard to hold. Its blade was dull and cheap, forcing her to strain as she peeled each apple. The image gnawed at Farber into the night. At 1:30 A.M., he picked up the phone and called Davin Stowell, a founder of the New York product development firm Smart Design, which had done a few projects for Copco. "He had this idea and he couldn't sleep," Stowell recalls.

90

The pair talked at length. It wasn't just about a peeler. It was a discussion about all sorts of cooking utensils, most of which were made as cheaply as possible with little thought given to comfort or ease of use. Farber believed that kitchen gadgets designed to be comfortable for sufferers of arthritis such as his wife would be just as appealing to the masses. He wanted to create ones that worked better for everyone.

He didn't know it at the time, but Farber was proselytizing Universal Design. It's the idea of creating products that are easy to use for the widest possible spectrum of customers— young and old; male and female; left- and right-handed; European, Asian, and American; and those with physical challenges such as arthritis. That's different from creating a gadget specifically for arthritic hands. Instead, Farber wanted to create a product line that considered as broad a range of needs as possible in the design process.

Smart Design went to work on a new peeler, and a handful of other products. Designers increased the diameter of the handle, which decreased hand strain. They settled on an oval shape with squared-off edges to help prevent slipping. They used an industrial rubber for the grip that was both safe for a dishwasher and wouldn't break down when exposed to cooking oils. And the blade was *sharp*.

Original OXO vegetable peeler.
(Courtesy of Smart Design)

91

Farber's industry connections helped him launch OXO, and when the peeler and the other fourteen products hit the market in 1990, they sold well from the start.

Universal Design remains at the heart of OXO to this day. While kitchen tools are still the company's core offerings, it has applied the ideas of Universal Design to gardening tools, cleaning gadgets, and office supplies. OXO has learned that outliers—arthritic cooks who have trouble gripping utensils, for example—are sensitive enough to spot design flaws that the rest of us unthinkingly accept.

Sound familiar? The outliers Nike relies on are professional athletes, such as skateboarder Paul Rodriguez. LEGO reached out to hard-core adult Mindstorms fans to help guide the design for the product's second generation. "Edges of a population can act as a litmus test for design," says Dan Formosa, one of the other Smart Design founders.

OXO's focus on Universal Design has helped the company's sales grow at a compounded annual rate of 27 percent since its birth. Even in the depths of the recession, at a time you might think consumers wouldn't shell out extra for its premium-priced goods, OXO continued to grow. The company, owned by personal-care products maker Helen of Troy Limited in El Paso, Texas, saw its sales jump 13 percent to $203.6 million in its fiscal 2010.

Universal Design is the reason there's a wall full of two hundred gloves of all shapes and sizes in the OXO kitchen. Over the years, employees have collected single gloves discovered during their travels to remind them of all the different hands for which they are creating products. There's a red mitten that once belonged to a child, and a weathered, half-finger cycling glove. And then there is a heavy-duty rubber fisherman's glove, pinned below a tag that reads:

When: August 30, 2001, 4:45 pm
Where: Prince Edward Island, Canada
Who: Alex

Alex is Alex Lee, the president of OXO. Born in Hong Kong, Lee moved to New York in 1980 to attend Parsons School of Design, where he earned a bachelor's degree in product design. He then joined the firm of Michael Graves, the celebrated architect and designer who gained recent fame for his line of domestic products sold at Target. There, Lee worked on several products for designer brands such as Alessi and Steelcase. He still uses the leather business-card holder he created for Graves's firm featuring a tab to pull the cards out easily.

But Lee wasn't ever quite happy at the firm. "I was the sole modernist among postmodernists," Lee says. He wanted to create products that were more functional and widely distributed than the ones the firm was designing. He debated with his boss so much that Lee says Graves gave him the nickname "Dr. No." It got Lee thinking beyond making the products. He wanted to create businesses. So he applied to Harvard Business School, earning his MBA in 1994. Farber hired him out of grad school to run the company when he re-retired. Lee took over management of OXO in 1996.

Lee meets me in a room at company headquarters set up

93

like a retail OXO display on steroids. The walls are packed with hundreds of OXO products, many items stocked ten deep. To his left are OXO's heat-resistant silicon spatulas in colors the company has dubbed key lime, blueberry, and cherry. Just over his shoulder rests OXO's upmarket SteeL line of barware, including its clever corkpull that opens wine bottles simply by turning the soft handle in the same direction until the cork pops out. On the display to Lee's right are the gardening supplies, such as the Outdoor Pour & Store watering can with a longneck spout that rotates 180 degrees to hug the two-gallon body for easy storage.

Lee, forty-nine, is wearing a pale blue oxford shirt, open at the collar, with crisp khaki trousers. His dark black hair has flecks of gray at the temples. As one of a handful of executives with degrees in both design and business, he understands more than most the imperative of using design to woo customers. And yet, he recognizes that as easy as it might be to describe OXO's methods, it would be nearly impossible to emulate them. "If you lay out the OXO process on a chart, it looks like everyone else's," Lee says. "The difference is the culture."

It's a culture that encourages employees to challenge one another's ideas. "I've been in big company meetings where everyone is cordial and polite," Lee says. "Then there's a bathroom break and someone says, 'That was bullshit.' I'm thinking, 'Why don't you say that in the meeting?'" That's what Lee has tried to promote at OXO. He works to create a culture where employees feel comfortable pursuing innovations even as their colleagues continually try to refine them. "The culture has to allow it to happen without it being personal," Lee explains.

94

When Lee took over OXO, he set the tone. "I was always the chief anal-retentive officer." He was the one who would look for flaws. He'd even pull out a high-powered magnifying glass to make sure the tiny OXO logo on the tooling samples—the first version of products rolling off the production line—looked right. Now, that sort of obsession is ingrained at OXO. "People here are looking for problems all the time," Lee says.

You might think this would make OXO employees more risk-averse, worried that their unformed, breakthrough ideas will get shot down. But it doesn't. OXO employees, who've worked at the company on average for five years, understand that the company's success depends on coming up with novel concepts rather than iterative products. "We try to promote calculated risks," Lee says.

OXO starts with a question: What frustrates consumers when they're working in the kitchen, the garden, the bathroom, their office? "Our process is finding a pet peeve," Lee says. "If there's no pet peeve, there's no product. It's just me-too." The pet peeve that launched the company was the discomfort of using a standard vegetable peeler. Like that vegetable peeler, many pet peeves are aggravations that consumers put up with without ever really knowing it. Design gurus often refer to these as unspoken needs.

OXO addressed one unspoken need with its angled measuring cups, one of a handful of ideas that came to the company from the outside. In June 1999, toy developers at Bang Zoom Design in Cincinnati recognized a problem in the way

95

OXO angled measuring cup.
(© 2010 OXO)

cooks use traditional measuring cups. Most folks fill them with a bit of liquid, then cock their heads sideways to read the measurements. Then they add a bit more liquid or pour some out to get just the right amount. Cooks didn't complain about it; that's just how it worked. "If you asked them what they wanted, they'd probably never tell you," Lee says.

The Bang Zoom developers created a measuring cup with markings on a ledge that wraps around the inside of the cup, angled upward from the base to the spout, that cooks could view from above as they poured. The prototype was raw—an opaque plastic cup with none of the visual or ergonomic touches for which OXO is known. But because that internal, angled ledge had measurement markings on it, cooks could see when they've poured, say, a cup just by looking down. With Smart Design, OXO refined the design, using transparent materials and adding a more comfortable handle. It became one of the fastest-selling products in OXO history.

OXO has a deep product line, some eight hundred strong, adding about a hundred new ones each year while cutting some thirty or forty nonperformers. That gives the company the luxury of being able to take its time with product development. It just isn't that dependent on having any one new product launch in any given year. "If we pull one product, it's not going to kill us," Lee says.

Take its LiquiSeal Travel Mug. There are plenty of travel mugs on the market. Just stop into Starbucks and you'll see shelffuls. But the pet peeve OXO recognized was that most of them spill easily. And the ones that don't make it a challenge to open in order to sip your morning coffee. "We wanted a mug that was watertight so you could throw it in your bag and it wouldn't spill," Lee says. What's more, consumers needed to be able to open and drink from it with one hand, so that they could drive at the same time.

OXO took its ideas to Smart Design in 1995, and after two years the companies produced a sealed mug that opened when users squeezed a lever near the top. Pretty clever. Lee was visiting the contract manufacturer in Taiwan when the tooling samples of the mug first appeared for testing. He poured hot water in to see how the mug worked. He held it upright, squeezed the lever, and the drinking hole opened. "Great," he thought. Then he closed the mug and tilted it away from him, figuring users might tip the mug before squeezing it and taking a sip. He squeezed the lever again. This time, scalding hot water shot across the room.

It was a lesson in physics. When the mug is held upright, the steam, which wants to escape from it, has nothing to block its path. But tilting the mug put liquid at the opening. The steam had to push through that liquid, propelling it out, in order to escape. The mug was a lawsuit waiting to happen.

97

"We killed the product," Lee says. But OXO didn't give up on solving the problem.

OXO and Smart Design went back to work, creating a chamber inside the mug that would release the air pressure before liquid would come out. The original mechanism for that approach was so unwieldy, though, that OXO scrapped it. The companies eventually decided to put a single button at the top of the mug, knowing that users would push the button and release the pressure before tilting the mug to drink. The first mugs hit store shelves in 2003, some eight years after OXO began development.

As the design process dragged on, OXO's investment piled up. Lee estimates that OXO and Smart Design both spent six figures developing the mug. "Our feeling was that we'd never see the return on investment," Lee says. "But if you spend the time to get it right, it pays off. We've seen the return plus." The mug has consistently ranked among OXO's top twenty best-selling items since it was introduced. OXO used clever design to turn an abysmal failure into one of its greatest successes.

Failures like the original travel mug have become a part of OXO's oral tradition. It would be wrong to suggest that the company celebrates mistakes, but when they inevitably happen, it embraces the opportunity to learn as much as possible from them. Think back to Nike's Mark Parker. Remember how he talked about how taking risks meant accepting the occasional failure? Well, that's part of OXO's DNA too. There are many companies that would rather move past their missteps, hoping no one really notices. When a screwup occurs, OXO shines a spotlight on the blunders, making sure that everyone at the company understands what went wrong.

Perhaps the most legendary misstep in OXO lore came in 1997, when it launched its take on the bagel slicer. Research had shown that folks were showing up at hospital emergency rooms in disproportionate numbers over the weekends with injuries sustained from cutting bagels. Knives would slice through the bagels and into the hands holding them. So OXO and Smart Design created a device with spring-loaded walls to hold the bagel firmly in place. Folks could grab a handle on the outside for stability, then slice the bagel down the middle, stopping at the polypropylene cutting-board base. When the first samples showed up in OXO's headquarters, they worked like a charm.

A few weeks later, Lee and category director Michelle Sohn, who had led the product development, were in Chicago to launch the bagel slicer at the annual International Home and Housewares Show, the key trade show of the kitchen gadget business. To prepare, they did a run-through of their presentation, putting Chicago's finest bagels through the slicer. But the bagels there aren't anything like New York bagels. They're smaller and denser. "Some of them I wouldn't call bagels," Sohn says. "They were a roll with a hole in it." The spring-loaded mechanism couldn't properly grasp those bagels, so they just spun around when they were being cut. "Immediately, it starts to hit you that, 'Oh, my God, there are different kinds of bagels from different parts of the country,'" Sohn says. "It was a total oversight." The printed marketing materials went in the trash. The booth space was filled with other products. The bagel slicer was shelved.

OXO, which prides itself on the idea of designing products for the widest possible audience, had focused too narrowly. It had never dawned on Sohn and her New York–based colleagues that bagels could vary so widely. "It's almost hard to imagine that it happened to us because we believe in Universal Design and forgot to look at bagels from other parts of the country," Sohn says.

Sohn may have been chastened, but she was never chastised. She remains one of OXO's most senior employees. And her misstep isn't uttered in hushed tones. It's cheerfully repeated as a cautionary tale. "Here was one of those times where we asked the wrong question," Lee says. "You set the wrong criteria and you get the wrong solution." For the next bagel-slicer iteration, OXO asked its sales representatives to ship in batches of bagels from around the country. Prototypes of other products now typically get sent to distributors around the world for local testing. "We'll never miss again like that," Sohn says.

More recently, OXO looked at jumping into the food-storage market, which companies such as Tupperware have defined for decades. OXO wondered if it could come up with a vacuum-sealed container. The first, ineffective iterations used pump mechanisms to suck out air.

The company stepped back a bit and rethought its original idea. "The question we asked was not quite correct," Lee says. "If you want to store sugar and flour, you don't really need a vacuum." What you need is an airtight container that stays shut, yet is easy for cooks to open. OXO turned to Form Co., a design firm in Japan, which Lee calls "the food-container capital of the world." Form came up with a container whose lid has a gasket around the brim that expands when users press a big button on its lid. That creates the airtight seal. Press the button again to retract the gasket. What's more, when the button pops up, it becomes a handle to open the container. OXO launched the Pop Container line in 2008, and five of the eleven different-size containers ranked among the company's top ten best-selling products that year.

OXO's success has led other companies to its door. In 2007, the giant office-supply retailer Staples came knocking, hoping to expand its own product offerings with a line that would help distinguish it from its rivals and build brand loyalty. So OXO and Smart Design pored over the product reviews on the Staples Web site, ferreting out customers' pet peeves.

One of the big ones was how staple removers tear paper. "Makes a mess of the paper when trying to pull out smaller staples," wrote one Erie, Pennsylvania, customer about a conventional staple remover in September 2007. OXO's first attempt at a solution looked a bit like a stick with a tongue and fangs hanging off the front. Users would slide the tongue under the staple, then press a button to extend the fangs and grasp it. Then, they would pry the staple out. It looked cool—but the paper still tore. "It was design for design's sake," says Michael Patel Delevante, a category director who oversaw the project.

Designers tinkered some more and came up with a much simpler gadget, a rubber handle attached to a long metal prong, resembling a letter opener. The prong is the width of a staple at the tip, and gradually gets both wider and thicker toward the base. When someone slides the prong under a staple, it disengages from the paper gradually as the metal bends outward.

101

OXO Good Grips staple remover. *(© 2010 OXO)*

The comments on the Staples Web site regarding the OXO staple remover are almost universally positive. "I work at the local County Clerk & Recorders office and I deal with stacks of paperwork all day, so I have a unique perspective on staple removers," writes one customer from Great Falls, Montana. "And you just can't beat this one for ease and reliability." And that's despite the fact that Staples sells it for $5.99, right next to a three-pack of the traditional clawlike staple removers for $2.99. I'll do the math for you; it's six times more expensive.

Like many companies that use design to avoid commoditization, OXO routinely charges premiums over competing goods. When those premiums for other companies' products run into the hundreds or even thousands of dollars, customers may think twice, particularly when economic times are tough. But because many OXO products sell for less than ten dollars, the premiums aren't particularly prohibitive. In the case of the staple remover, it's not much more than the price of a latte. It's much easier for a consumer to dig a little deeper for OXO's products because they don't have to dig too deep. What's more, retailers are willing to promote products that offer them more margin. "They'd rather sell a hundred thousand units of something at ten dollars than a hundred thousand units at eight dollars," Lee says. The staple remover quickly became OXO's second-best-selling product at Staples, behind its three-hole punch.

Pursuing this rigorous path toward the right design takes guts. "We have a lot of companies that come to us and say, 'Do for us what you did for OXO,'" says Smart Design's Dan Formosa. "I tell them, 'I don't think you have the nerve.'" OXO's approach often increases product development costs fivefold, he says. It puts a great deal of weight on intuition rather than traditional market research. And it relies on the marketplace, not focus groups, to validate its ideas.

That's not to say that their product-development process is haphazard. OXO follows a formal design process, very similar to the one LEGO uses. It begins with Phase 0, what LEGO calls P0. It's an exploratory stage in which the company puts together a design brief, anywhere from four to fifteen pages, laying out the problem it wants solved, potential product features, and target price points. Then it hands the brief over to Smart Design, Form, or one of seven other design firms with which it works. The phase often concludes with a brainstorming session, where OXO and the design firm conjure up product concepts.

Phase 1 is the concepting stage, in which OXO and its design partner start refining their work. Designers start sketching product ideas. They consider different materials.

103

And they build models, often "Frankenstein" creations cobbled together from spare parts lying around the office. The idea of using a soft silicone for the company's successful Silicone Sink Strainer came from a soft muffin mold that was sitting on a desk at Smart Design. The folks there cut it apart, popped a few holes in one of the cups, and put a screw through the center of it to use as a post to pull it out of the drain. Because the material is flexible, it's easy to invert to remove debris over a trash can. Those basic models help OXO answer the question of whether the product will address the unspoken need.

If it does, the company moves to Phase 2, in which it designs and develops the product. Here, designers use 3-D modeling programs to create their gizmos. They work with engineers at OXO to figure out what will and won't work. "It's not uncommon for us to get to Phase 2 in the design process and go back to Phase 1," says Larry Witt, OXO's senior vice president of sales and market development.

When an idea moves to Phase 3, OXO and its designers refine the concept even more, ultimately creating a tooling mold that its manufacturers will use to build the first samples. With those samples, the company tests the products to see if they actually do what was intended. This is the stage where the original travel mug failed. When the products work, though, it's off to manufacturing.

On paper, it's all very similar to LEGO's design process—and that of scores of other companies. What makes OXO—and LEGO for that matter—successful is, as Lee says, the company culture. OXO employees instinctively look for those unmet needs, through careful and frequent user observation, and push their design firm partners to create products that meet them.

OXO's approach won't work for every company. Take its decision to outsource design. That requires OXO to manage relationships with each of the nine different design firms with which it works. And there's nothing conventional about those interactions. The firms aren't hired merely to put a sheen on a nearly finished product. Instead, they work hand-in-glove with OXO on consumer research, observing consumers working in their kitchens, gardens, and bathrooms. Rather than receiving a fee, the firms get a 3 percent royalty on each product they help create—the same deal Farber struck with Smart Design at OXO's dawn.

Back then, it made sense to use outside designers to keep costs down. As the company has grown, Lee has considered hiring designers in-house. He figures the company could employ as many as twenty designers and keep them all busy and still have work for its contract firms. But he hasn't yet done it. Lee worries that design decision making would become hierarchical. And he frets that in-house designers would grab the most obvious winning ideas, leaving the more challenging designs to outsiders. That, in turn, would discourage the other firms from working with the company. For now, OXO continues to rely on the design brilliance of others.

Over the years, OXO has moved from the kitchen to the garden to the bathroom to the office. Lee insists that the concepts of Universal Design will allow OXO to stretch its brand even further. "Every time I go to a dinner and say what I do, inevitably someone says, 'You know what OXO should make?'" Lee says. Often, they want garage door openers or hand trucks for moving boxes.

OXO hasn't done any of those products yet. But as we speak, Lee is preparing OXO for its most ambitious expansion to date. He's pushing the company into the hugely competitive baby-products business with a new product line called Tot.

The company will make everything from sippy cups with angled, nonslip handles—so children don't have to twist their wrists too much—to a tub kneeling mat made of dense foam with a loop to hang it on a hook behind the door. Lee is betting that the Tot line will appeal to many of the same young, urban consumers who buy OXO's other products for the kitchen or bathroom. He thinks it could evolve into a $50-million-a-year business for the company.

It's only recently that OXO even considered doing baby products. For the first fifteen years of its existence, OXO's staff was, by and large, young and childless. "If I told these people to do Tot six years ago, it would have been a flop," Lee says. But in the last five years, its eighty-four employees have had twenty-six babies. "All of a sudden, there are a thousand pet peeves," Lee says. And for OXO, that just might be enough for a real business.

5

REI

I'm about halfway up the Pinnacle. It's my second climb on this Seattle spring morning. Truth be told, it's my second time rock climbing in nearly a decade. Down below, some thirty or forty feet, Day Frostenson has me on belay; that is, he's holding the other end of the rope that's attached to my harness. If I fall, he's going to make sure I don't drop too far.

So far, I haven't put him to work. Frostenson is encouraging me to push with my legs and not pull with my arms. I know, I know. But I'm not really doing it. And as I haul myself over the last bit of a not particularly challenging overhang sixty feet or so above him, my arms are rubbery and I'm ready for a break. I rappel back down.

I flash back nearly three decades. Back then, I was a teenager enamored with rock and ice climbing. I'd scaled some sheer rock walls on upstate New York's Shawangunk

Ridge, and in the summer of 1980, I'd learned to use an ice ax and crampons. By August, I'd picked my way to the top of Glacier Peak in Washington State. There's a terrific sense of accomplishment summiting a peak, particularly a 10,541-foot one such as Glacier Peak, when spent muscles quiver and the sweat that poured out during the climb becomes chilly in the high-altitude winds. It's a feeling that comes when you realize that you're standing on a spot where few have been or would dare to go. You become part of an exclusive club.

As a sixteen-year-old kid, I gave little thought to design. I hadn't studied how products were created, stores were laid out, or services were offered. Like most consumers, I was a shopper, not a student of business strategy. I had become a mountaineer and, when I went to buy gear, I shopped at Recreational Equipment Inc. Why there? Looking back, I see in me what I describe in previous chapters about the other companies' customers. REI, as the Seattle-based outdoor outfitter is known to its customers, gave me something I didn't know I wanted. It didn't just sell me gear; it offered authenticity. It was the store where mountaineers went to buy their ropes, harnesses, and boots. Sure, they could find trusted goods there. But they also went to REI because it was a place where they could trade stories with the staff or ask for advice, knowing they'd get a valuable opinion. Just like summiting Glacier Peak, shopping at REI placed me among a group of people with whom I wanted to be identified.

Back to the Pinnacle I just climbed. It's not a rock face in a national or state park. It's not even a pale imitation of Glacier Peak. It's man-made—the highest freestanding climbing structure in the nation when it was built in 1996. There are twenty possible routes up the sixty-five-foot spire, and I've managed to scale two of the easier ones—routes climbers would rate 5.5 and 5.7, meaning they have only a bit of technical difficulty. From the top, I can see the snowcaps on the

REI Pinnacle, Seattle. *(Courtesy of REI)*

REI

Olympic Mountains just over the tops of office buildings in Seattle. I'm seeing them through the floor-to-ceiling plate-glass panels because I'm inside. I repel down, take off my harness, and enter the world of Recreational Equipment Inc.

REI may be one of the best companies at turning shopping into an experience and turning customers into devoted patrons. That's because REI isn't merely a place to pick up parkas, tents, or bikes. It's a store where customers can go to learn how to use a GPS device on a trail, figure out which local waterways offer the best kayaking for beginners, and discover what to pack for a summit attempt on a fourteen-thousand-foot peak. It's a place where outdoor enthusiasts go to be inspired.

REI sits at the crossroads of industrial design and service design. It makes luggage, sleeping bags, and tents that are perennial award winners from the outdoor press. It's big on fashion design. It may not be haute couture, but everything from its parkas and socks to its pants, sweaters, and shorts are worn as much in the city as on the trail. But the type of design that really sets REI apart from rivals is experiential. REI offers a shopping experience with a fiercely loyal following among customers.

In fact, many of its customers, some ten million of them, have become members over the years. You don't have to be a member to shop at REI. But if you are a member, you get a dividend at the end of the year based on how much you bought. Typically, it amounts to about 10 percent of all non-sale purchases. Plenty of retailers have formal and informal memberships that offer discounted goods—everything from the plastic card that lets you in the door at Costco Wholesale so you can buy toilet paper in bulk, to the dog-eared punch card you get from the neighborhood coffee shop that gives you a free latte after you've purchased ten.

But this cooperative is bigger than the kind you might find at a community organic market. In fact, it is the biggest consumer cooperative in the country, with 3.7 million active members, folks who have spent ten dollars or more in the previous year. The dividend induces members to join. But it also gives them a piece of the business. REI has done what most retailers can only dream of. "They created a cult," says frog design president Doreen Lorenzo. There's that word again—*cult*. Remember? That's what Porsche works so hard to create around its cars, so much so that its customers form fan clubs. Nike's fetishist sneakerheads camp outside stores to be first in line for limited-edition shoes. You see LEGO's cult at every BrickFest. And here, REI has created a $1.4-billion-a-year cult, with more than 110 stores in twenty-seven states and the District of Columbia.

To those in the club, there's even a bit of competition over having the lowest number, because the co-op hands out member numbers sequentially. The lower the number, the longer the membership. Of those ten million members, Mary Anderson is the longest tenured. Member number 2, she founded the cooperative with her husband, Lloyd, member number 1, in 1938. REI won't break out specifics regarding single-digit-numbered members, or, for that matter, double-digit and triple-digit members. The co-op will say only that plenty still shop at REI regularly, though some may be using their parents' or grandparents' membership cards.

I joined the co-op as a teenager back on New Year's Day,

1981. That was a few months after I conquered Glacier Peak. That makes me number 1,042,873, an inglorious seven-digit, like the vast majority of REI members. But at least I'm a low seven-digit. The point of the game is to show just how authentic an outdoors person you are, because REI, after all, was there at the very earliest days of mountaineering.

Back in the 1920s and 1930s, long before "peak bagging" became mountaineer argot for reaching the summit of as many mountains as possible, Lloyd Anderson was a peak bagger extraordinaire. In 1930, he climbed the 6 highest peaks in Washington State in a three-month span, the first to ever achieve the feat in just one summer. According to Harvey Manning's folksy 1988 history, *REI: 50 Years of Climbing Together*, Anderson bagged 145 peaks from 1935 to 1945, and another 108 summits in the 1950s. After conquering the snow-capped mountains of the Pacific Northwest, Anderson moved on to mountains in Mexico such as Popocatepetl and Ixtaccihuatl, and alpine summits such as Jungfrau and the Matterhorn.

In 1935, Anderson was in need of a good ice ax. His earlier summits were aided by only an alpenstock, a glorified walking stick. The best deal on an ice ax he could find locally, at a shop run by a guy named Eddie Bauer, would have cost him nearly $17.50. Another Seattle store sold axes for twenty bucks. Those were heady sums, more money than Anderson, an engineer with the Seattle Transit System, cared to part with.

So Anderson kept shopping and, at a friend's suggestion, looked through European magazines that carried ads for outdoor stores. Anderson saw one for Sporthaus Peterlong, a gear store in Innsbruck, Austria, and requested a catalog. When it arrived, it was, of course, in German. But Mary, his wife, knew enough of the language to translate the product descriptions, leading her husband to a top-notch ax that he bought for all of $3.50, postage included.

It was a revelation, and Anderson wanted to both find more such deals on climbing gear and share his good fortune with his mountaineering buddies. He began facilitating purchases for others, picking up pitons and more ice axes from Germany. By 1938, it had become enough of a business that he decided to make it official. The Andersons found twenty-one other mountaineering cohorts, and each contributed one dollar to form the Recreational Equipment Cooperative, known back then simply as the Co-op. The genesis was that first ice ax, which is why the handles on the front doors of every REI store are fashioned from ice axes.

The fact that Anderson created a cooperative—one that distributes more than half of the profits generated by member merchandise purchases as dividends, more than $770 million over the years—says much about the customer-experience design of REI that lives to this day. Anderson could have started a regular for-profit business, and kept as much of those profits as he liked. But Anderson just wanted to be outdoors, and he wanted his climbing partners to have the same high-quality gear that he had. That altruistic ethic has paradoxically been great for business. In those early days, mountaineers from the Northwest flocked to the Co-op because the guy who ran the place was one of them. He loved the outdoors and wanted others to enjoy it with him. It wasn't until 1947 that Anderson took his first paycheck from the Co-op, an annual 5 percent commission that totaled $1,185.70.

There's a lot of corporate history there. And it would be easy to get caught up in the story of REI and forget about its design chops. So let's think about the story again. A hard-core climber, the fringe customer who understands the needs of climbers intimately, is frustrated by the mountaineering stores of the day. So what does he do? He designs the store that he wants. Turns out that other mountaineers want the exact same thing. Familiar? Ferry Porsche launched his car company because he couldn't find the car of his dreams. Phil Knight and Bill Bowerman created Nike to sell affordable, high-performance running shoes that weren't available anywhere else. Sam Farber's arthritic wife struggled with a vegetable peeler, so he decided to design one that would be more comfortable for everyone to use. Add Lloyd Anderson to that list.

And just as those other companies are part of the fabric of their industries, REI is steeped in the history of climbing. It has outfitted some legendary expeditions, such as Peter Habeler's and Reinhold Messner's 1978 Mount Everest climb without supplemental oxygen and the 1980 American women's expedition to Dhaulagiri in the Himalayas. And just about every great American mountaineer, certainly in the early days of climbing, was an REI member. Some even worked for the cooperative. The most famous of them is Anderson's protégé, Jim Whittaker. A legend in climbing circles, Whittaker was the first American to summit Mount Everest, a feat he achieved in 1963. That led to a trip to the White House to receive congratulations from President

John F. Kennedy, which in turn led to a deep friendship with the Kennedy clan, particularly with Robert F. Kennedy, for whom Whittaker was a pallbearer.

Years before he scaled Everest, Whittaker was Anderson's student, then his partner. In his memoir, *A Life on the Edge*, Whittaker writes of Independence Day, 1950, when the two of them climbed to the crater atop Mount Rainier and set off fireworks their friends could see all the way from Seattle, fifty-five miles to the north. Their friendship and Whittaker's passion for the outdoors led Anderson to offer him the job of running the Co-op when it got too big for him to manage while holding down his day job.

Back then, the cooperative had about six thousand members, roughly eighty thousand dollars in annual sales, and a tiny second-floor walk-up retail space just above the Green Apple Pie restaurant in downtown Seattle (long since shuttered). Whittaker took the job, stocking shelves, sweeping floors, and shipping packages. In between, he offered advice to customers about mountaineering, and swapped stories about hikes and climbs.

REI became a climber's climbing store. Under Whittaker, the Co-op set up its own testing department to gauge the reliability of the carabiners, pitons, and ropes it sold. It also started selling its own private-label down goods, offering lower-priced parkas and sleeping bags while retaining more profit. And it began donating money to environmental causes, embracing wilderness conservation as part of its mission.

117

That outdoorsy authenticity is an ethos that remains with REI to this day, even though its customer base has grown far broader. The vast majority of REI's customers these days aren't trying to bag peaks in the manner of Lloyd Anderson. Many are looking for a warm down coat for the winter or a comfortable pair of hiking boots when the weather turns warm. But by staying true to that fringe, hard-core customer, REI has designed a store—really, it has crafted an experience— that makes customers trust it as a valued purveyor of outdoor gear. The goal of getting people to go outside drives every decision at the cooperative. "REI is a purpose-driven place and design helps us achieve that purpose," says president and chief executive Sally Jewell. And that, in turn, makes REI the kind of store where the sixteen-year-old climber-wannabe version of me as well as the middle-aged outdoorsy version of me wants to spend time and money. It's the key to great service design: Create an experience that reflects customers, or, better still, an ideal in which customers would like to see themselves.

Jewell may not be a peak bagger on the order of Anderson or Whittaker, but she's planning to summit Mount Rainier twice in the coming months. It's a peak she first conquered as a sixteen-year-old. She's an avid cross-country skier, sailor, and rock climber, a recreational cyclist, and she loves to camp. When I sit down with her, Jewell is wearing khaki hiking pants and a white T-shirt under an REI shell jacket. She wears her silver-and-black hair short and no-fuss.

Because REI is a cooperative, Jewell doesn't have Wall Street breathing down her neck to make the next quarter's numbers. But, of course, selling gear is important. "There's no mission without margin," Jewell likes to say. "We have to run a healthy business." But it's really the mission of

118

educating and inspiring customers to go outside that fuels the business. That's why every REI offers free clinics covering everything from bike maintenance to orienteering with maps and compasses. Customers shopping for, say, a tent can grab a richly detailed pamphlet explaining the different features and offering a side-by-side comparison of the weight, dimensions, and price of the dozens of tents it sells.

That's one reason REI designs its own gear, even as it sells products from other companies. The cooperative stands behind everything it sells, no matter the manufacturer. But it also wants to offer quality gear at prices many of its suppliers can't touch. So it has an in-house design staff of eight, and relies on guys like David Mydans, a senior product designer, to create products that resonate with customers.

Mydans, who has been designing products for REI since 1986, is a self-described "dirtbag climbing bum," a scraggly graybeard who spends upward of sixty days every year sleeping in a tent. "I like to lie in a tent late in the afternoon, when the sun is low in the sky, and see the architecture of the tent," he says.

Back in 2006, Mydans obsessed over REI's three-person Quarter Dome tent, a popular model for backpackers who want to travel light. At four pounds seven ounces, it's not much to strap onto a backpack and haul through the woods. But Mydans wanted to make it bigger without adding weight. He couldn't figure out how to do it with the tried-and-true frame of two crisscrossing tent poles holding the tent upright.

Until one day, after drawing sketch after sketch of new tent designs, he visualized a new structure. It wasn't a

119

moment of epiphany as much as it was a result of obsessive tinkering. "I saw it before I built it," Mydans says. His novel design used only one full-length tent pole, arching diagonally from one corner of the tent to another. Instead of crossing that first pole with a matching one, Mydans came up with an altogether novel idea: He'd use two shorter poles, coming up from opposite corners. Instead of connecting in the middle, those poles would angle outward, stopping slightly off center about two-thirds of the way across the tent. The new design increased the interior volume of the tent by 34 percent, and even shaved seven ounces off the weight.

There was still one problem: Mydans wasn't certain the structure would hold, particularly in a driving rain with blustery winds. His solution was to stitch trusses into the tent that use tension in order to keep the shorter poles in place and the tent sturdy. The inspiration came from Buckminster Fuller's Tensegrity structures, which use tension to create structural integrity. The day REI tested the tent in a wind tunnel, where a handful of Mydans's design colleagues gathered, he was apprehensive. "If this thing had blown down in relatively low wind speeds, it would have been back to the drawing board," Mydans says. He pitched the prototype and watched as the winds blew at twenty-five miles per hour. The tent cupped in the gust, then popped right back into shape. "Yes!" Mydans recalls blurting, punctuating it with a fist pump. "I can be pretty emotional."

The payoff: The tent won the Editor's Choice award from *Backpacker* magazine. That helped boost sales 162 percent from the previous season's sales of the old Quarter Dome tent. All because Mydans was fixated. "Necessity is the

REI Quarter Dome tent. *(Courtesy of REI)*

mother of expediency. Obsession is the mother of invention," Mydans says.

To be fair, several other outdoor companies do great design as well, sharing the same passion for products. Just as Mydans came up with the unusual structure for the Quarter Dome, designers at Marmot Mountainworks conjured up a similar approach for that company's Aura tent. And that won *Outside* magazine's Gear of the Year award.

But Mydans's obsession speaks volumes about REI's design approach. REI's seven other designers have that same obsession for their outdoor pursuits. They climb and hike, ski and bike, and do so with the same zeal that Mydans does. And because they are at the extreme, the hardest of hard-core users, they see things other designers might miss. They instinctively understand the shortcomings of existing gear. And as they design that award-winning gear, they create the aura of authenticity for which customers yearn.

The cooperative doesn't exist to create climbing gear; its mission is to get people outside. If the prevailing price for lightweight backpacking tents is prohibitive, it jumps into the market to fill that need. It's laser-focused on the business of helping folks enjoy nature.

Perhaps more than any other piece of REI's business, store layout is the quintessential REI design skill. It's in the stores that REI customers come to know the cooperative. And the stores have come a long way from the 1930s, when the Co-op was not much more than a shelf at a farmers' market, or even the 1950s, when Jim Whittaker ran the shop above the Green Apple Pie.

The Pinnacle I climbed was once a key piece of REI's efforts to bring the climbing experience to its customers. Back when it debuted in 1996, there were few indoor climbing facilities at all, let alone a sixty-five-foot man-made boulder to ascend. REI built a second Pinnacle in 2000 in its Denver store. Another twenty-six stores have free-standing pinnacles, and a handful of others have smaller climbing walls.

These days, though, the Seattle Pinnacle is more of a tourist destination than anything else. "We probably won't build a lot more Pinnacles," says Dean Iwata, REI director of store development. "When we first started, it was totally unique." Now it's not unusual to see climbing walls in hotels, schools, and health clubs. Seattle, like many large cities, has a handful of climbing gyms where serious climbers go to work on their technique. Frostenson, my belayer, who spent time climbing in Yosemite and the Tetons, told me that most of the Pinnacle climbers he ropes up are out-of-towners making a pilgrimage to the flagship store.

There was a time when REI thought it needed to turn its stores into virtual amusement parks for woodsy types. In addition to the Pinnacle, REI once had a rain room in its Seattle store where customers could get doused trying raincoats. Its Denver store once had a cold room where temperatures dipped to 0 degrees Fahrenheit, giving shoppers an unusual opportunity to compare the warmth of various parkas. "They were entertaining," Iwata says. "But we're not trying to re-create the outdoors indoors. We're trying to get people outdoors."

So REI is prototyping a new store design, and doing it on a grand scale. The process began in 2005 by imagining what the cooperative's stores might look like in ten years. Working with San Francisco architecture firm Gensler, REI managers visited stores that have become iconic for their brands. They were impressed by the way Apple offers classes to customers in its stores, and the way Whole Foods conveys the quality of its groceries with earthy colors and curved aisles that encourage shoppers to linger. The store designs are an extension of those companies' brands.

When it came time for REI to ponder what its future stores should look like, it started with a whiteboard exercise, jotting down words that represent REI's brand. *Entertainment* was a word that came up, but it was dispatched pretty quickly. The words that resonated most were *community* and *interaction,* words that reflect the approach that Lloyd Anderson and Jim Whittaker took with the first customers,

123

even if they never used the words. "We kept coming back to, how do the stores integrate into the community?" Iwata explains. "How do they inspire people?" Then, as now, customers came to REI not just for gear but for advice, education, and ideas. It's something that separates REI from its rivals, and Iwata wanted to bring it front and center.

Often when companies prototype a product they quickly throw it together—rapid prototyping—in order to test how the form might affect the product's function. Then it's tweaked and reworked and tested again. And for product design, that's as it should be. REI took that approach as far as it could with its store design, tinkering with new fixtures, lighting, and flooring in a one-thousand-square-foot warehouse space near the cooperative's headquarters. But when it comes to prototyping an entire store, you can slap together only so much.

So REI took the bold step of creating a working prototype—a 41,000-square-foot store in Boulder, Colorado, that opened in 2007. The store gets much recognition for its environmental friendliness, having earned a Leadership in Energy and Environmental Design, or LEED, gold certification from the U.S. Green Building Council. "That resonates with our customers," Iwata says.

As store manager Ali Bennett walks me through the Boulder outlet before it opens one sunny spring morning, I'm struck by how bright the place is, even though is has only a handful of lights turned on. That's because much of the store's light comes from nearly two hundred Solatubes, huge cylinders that direct daylight into the store. It uses a photovoltaic system to generate electricity, and high-efficiency plumbing fixtures to reduce water use. The rubber flooring

124

is made of recycled postconsumer and postproduction waste, and many of the display fixtures use Plyboo, a plywoodlike material made from highly renewable bamboo.

As important as all of this is to REI customers, who expect the cooperative to be as green as the Cascade Mountains in which it was born, it's the community center that was the most daring addition. Many REI stores have community rooms already. But often, as with the huge space almost hidden on the second floor of its Seattle flagship location, the room is tucked out of sight. When REI offers an avalanche clinic or a lecture from a renowned mountaineer at the Seattle store, it goes largely unnoticed by shoppers who hadn't previously heard about the event. In Boulder, the cooperative built a one-thousand-square-foot community room right in the middle of the store and visible throughout.

With the prototype, REI realized it didn't get the community center quite right. Designers had elevated the community room four feet above the rest of the store, figuring it would highlight the space, luring customers to it. But it made the room seem less approachable. Shoppers often hesitate before going up the stairs, unsure if the space is meant for employees only. "Instead of being a welcoming environment, it was an intimidating one," Jewell says.

Missteps, of course, are the whole point of a prototype. "If you don't make some mistakes, you're probably not doing your job," Iwata says. "You're not reaching for the boundaries." (This far into the book, that sentiment should start sounding familiar.) When REI opened its second prototype store in Round Rock, Texas, in 2008, it had a multifloor layout to work with. There, it put the 750-square-foot community center at the mezzanine level, between the two floors of retail space, forcing shoppers to walk through the center as they moved upstairs through the store.

The cooperative won't disclose the cost of the prototype stores. And the Round Rock store is still too new to gain any meaningful insight from its sales data. But REI executives say that sales from the Boulder store are ahead of projections. Is that because of the new store design? It's hard to tell. But there are some other indications that suggest the effort is worth the cost. Without disclosing specific figures, REI says that a larger percentage of customers are signing up for the twenty-dollar lifetime membership at the Boulder store than at the average REI outlet. And it has found that members are visiting the Boulder location more frequently than they did prior to the redesign.

It's hard to overestimate the loyalty that REI's community building engenders. You can even see it online, where members do more than just shop for gear and review products. They share experiences. Folks like "Mac . . . Again from New Mexico," the handle of a satisfied shopper who felt compelled to offer more than just his praise for the ninety-nine-dollar Jetboil Personal Cooking System's ability to boil water quickly, even at altitudes higher than ten thousand feet. Mac also decided to share a recipe for his very own "Dirt Road Chicken Chili," featuring kidney beans, tomato soup, chili powder, and chicken.

To be honest, it took REI a while to appreciate the power of its social network. Its Web site, like most retailers' online offerings, existed largely to sell goods. Sure, you could find store directions, clinic schedules, and press releases. When it launched product reviews in the summer of 2007, it was flooded with ten thousand in the first month. Later, it sent out an e-mail to a hundred thousand customers proposing a forum for outdoor photography. Within a few weeks, more than thirty-five hundred digital shots hit the REI in-box. "People are passionate about the things we do," says Jordan Williams, the manager of REI's online community and content development.

It's the same sort of passion Lloyd Anderson had when he started the cooperative. Though he passed away in 2000, his wife, Mary, still visits REI headquarters on special occasions. I got to see her at the annual Anderson Awards, given to rank-and-file workers who exemplify REI's core values—things like being true to the outdoors and providing trustworthy products and services. It's early December, a day after Anderson celebrated her ninety-ninth birthday. Jewell introduces her as "the mother of REI, the mother of all our jobs and our future." As Anderson's wheelchair is pushed onto a makeshift stage, the room gives her a standing ovation. "I didn't know I was the mother of all kinds of things," says Anderson, still feisty though frail.

The line gets a good laugh from a room that might otherwise be a tough crowd. It's the beginning of what will turn out to be one of the worst Christmases for retailers in decades. REI is hardly immune. A day before heading to its headquarters in an industrial park area in the Seattle suburb of Kent, I stop by the Seattle flagship store to pick up a gift for my wife. The store isn't quite empty, but it's hardly the bustling pre-Christmas frenzy that I remember from holidays past.

Jewell acknowledges as much to the troops. "This weekend stunk," she says that Monday morning. But in the face of a brutal retail environment, Jewell is buoyed by the awards ceremony. "There's nothing like the Anderson Awards to remind us why we're here," she tells her coworkers. The cooperative, after all, was founded by folks who just wanted to do fun activities outside. Jewell points to the gray sky outside the cafeteria's floor-to-ceiling windows. "It's cloudy. It's chilly. There's snow at the pass," she says enthusiastically. Sluggish sales can bring her down for only so long.

6

CLIF BAR

It's not quite six A.M. on a cool September morning in Pope Valley, California. The air is crisp and damp with the late-summer dew. The leaves rustle with the breezes that waft through the hills. At this isolated ranch in the mountains north of Napa Valley, the sun isn't up yet. And it's hard to say that the nearly two dozen folks assembled here are either. Except for Gary Erickson.

Indeed, it's hard to imagine Erickson ever at rest. An intense, kinetic man, Erickson runs Clif Bar & Company, the energy foods company he founded in 1992. The story is the stuff of legend among Clif Bar workers. Erickson had been a baker, a designer of bike saddles, and an amateur bicycle racer. In 1990, he went on a 175-mile ride with a buddy, jamming six PowerBars—the energy food of choice back then— into the back pocket of his cycling jersey. Nearly 120 miles and five PowerBars into the ride, he realized he just couldn't

stomach another taffylike energy snack. So he hightailed it to the nearest 7-Eleven, bought a box of powdered doughnuts, and scarfed down the entire box.

It was then that Erickson decided he could do better. That bike ride, the genesis of Clif Bar, is known at the company as the Epiphany Ride. Every year, Erickson celebrates it with his employees, though the course these days is different from the original route.

This year, the ride leaves from his sprawling 130-acre ranch, where he grows organic fruits and vegetables and raises goats, chickens, and turkeys, a far cry from the garage he lived in when he did the first Epiphany Ride. Employees who want to ride can choose from various routes of 30 to 150 miles over the roads in Napa and Yolo counties. There's no doubt which route Erickson is taking. And I'm with him, astride my road bike, picking up Erickson's silhouette as he bounds out of his ranch house at six A.M. and loudly greets the bleary-eyed riders:

"Let's go! C'mon, everyone. Let's get started."

The first thing anyone riding with Erickson will realize is that the man is freakishly strong, particularly for a guy who, as CEO of a 230-employee company, can't be spending too much time in the saddle. But Erickson, whose fifty-first birthday is just three days away, has calves the size of grapefruits. And when he hits the first hills near Lake Berryessa, he's powering up near the front of a pretty elite pack of cyclists. How elite? Well, in addition to the collection of amateur racers and competitive athletes who work at Clif, there are a few professional riders whom the company sponsors along for the journey.

At the top of that list is Georgia Gould, a twenty-eight-year-old cyclist who competed on the U.S. mountain biking team at the Beijing Olympics just a month earlier. Gould, who finished eighth in Beijing, joked at the end of the Epiphany Ride that she thought it was going to be a casual spin where folks chatted and took long breaks for food and rest. Instead, Erickson helped push an inspired pace, zipping along at twenty-five to thirty miles an hour on flat roads and attacking steep climbs as though they were hills in the suburbs.

But riding 150 miles on a bike while climbing ten thousand feet isn't just about machismo. Sure, there's some of that, and plenty of smack talk during the ride. But the ride—just like the bevy of other athletic activities pursued by Clif employees—is a window into the key ingredient to Clif's success: It shows the company's authenticity. There's that word again. Just listen to Erickson. "I created a product for myself," he says. That concept should be starting to sound familiar by now. Ferry Porsche, Lloyd Anderson, and now Gary Erickson. They all created a product or service that met a need of theirs, which they couldn't get met anywhere else. When it comes to doing great design, authenticity matters and few companies really have it.

Let's pause here and revisit the word *design*. For too many companies, design starts and ends with aesthetics. But that's too narrow. Steve Jobs reminded us in the Introduction that design is how a product or service works. Porsche sweats how its 911 corners at high speeds. Nike puts more padding in the tongues of its skateboard shoes to cushion the inevitable blows from the board during tricks. Pay attention in this chapter to the way Clif develops products that improve its

133

customers' athletic performance. Clif doesn't merely develop products; it designs them and the experiences of using them. And it's an example of how the lessons of design can be applied to industries where aesthetics don't matter.

Clif makes great products in large part because its employees regularly use them. As cyclists, runners, triathletes, rock climbers, skiers, and participants in just about any other outdoor activity you can imagine, they know what their customers want because they are customers. They understand what it is to bonk—to run out of energy—125 miles into a bike ride because they've done it. They know what it's like for marathoners to struggle with chewing and swallowing energy foods during a race because they can't simultaneously take in enough oxygen. "Clif's story is authentic. It was born in an athletic environment," says Lanny Vincent, an innovation guru who has worked with Clif since 1998. This approach has fueled Clif's 25 percent annual sales growth through much of the last decade, with revenue now topping $200 million a year.

It all starts with Erickson. When you see the man, you realize he's more fit than slender. It's easy to believe that his gleaming bald head is a function of aerodynamics, not genetics. I visit with him again a month after the Epiphany Ride. He has just returned from Maui, where he competed in the 2008 XTERRA World Championship, a grueling off-road triathlon that attracts six hundred pro and amateur athletes. Erickson finished in 3 hours, 51 minutes, and 42 seconds, good enough for 225th place overall and 9th in the fifty- to fifty-four-year-old age group.

■ ■ ■

After his powdered-doughnut binge in 1990, Erickson went to his mother's kitchen and baked. He used natural ingredients, not the processed ones found in many of the energy bars of the day, because the baker in him knew the taste would be better and the nutritional benefits greater. He wanted a cookie texture because the cyclist in him knew that breathless riders would find it easier to chew and swallow. He spent months tinkering, burning out the motor of his mother's mixer in the process.

Since then, Clif has expanded well beyond the original bar. It's been the chief innovator in an industry that used to believe that cramming the maximum number of carbs down your gullet was all that really mattered. Right in the heart of its Berkeley headquarters sits the Mary Erickson Test Kitchen, named for the CEO's mother, who helped bake the first Clif Bar. The huge room is half kitchen and half science lab. There are industrial-grade ovens and stoves alongside scales that measure down to the 1/1000th of a gram and pipettes with ingredients to add just the slightest tweak of flavoring.

When I visit, the folks in Clif's R&D department are preparing a lunch for one another. Today's menu is Asian-themed, with one group making vegetarian rolls while another puts the finishing touches on a pear salad. The group is constantly encouraged to experiment, even while making lunch. Later in the day, they'll take a field trip to a vodka distiller and learn how it creates new varieties. They are challenged to play with new taste combinations, new food concepts. The idea is to expand their thinking beyond sports nutrition so that they'll experiment. Iterative products are fine, but the folks at Clif believe that experimentation will help it come up with breakthrough products as well.

The kitchen is at the center of Clif headquarters, both physically and metaphorically. It's the place where the food scientists and athletes who work at the company overturn the conventional wisdom about energy foods. The kitchen is the birthplace of Clif Quench, its all-natural sports drink that has no artificial flavors, colors, or preservatives. It's where Clif's baker-athletes have created Shot Roks protein bites to help with muscle recovery after workouts, and Kid Organic Twisted Fruit, Twizzler-shaped healthy snacks for children.

The kitchen's biggest design breakthrough came in 1999, when the company launched Luna bars, the energy bars created specifically for women, featuring extra calcium and folic acid. The company has always been active in grassroots marketing, sponsoring running and cycling events where it hands out product samples and stays in touch with its customers. Back in the late 1990s, it kept hearing the same complaint from women athletes: Many liked the flavor and texture of Clif Bars but didn't want so many calories. And several thought it would be nice to have a bar that was nutritionally fortified to meet women's needs, increasing the amount of iron, for example. "Women were feeling left out," says Michelle Ferguson, Clif's senior vice president of brand marketing and a foodie-athlete herself, with degrees in agricultural economics and an Ironman finish under her belt.

That's a key to Clif's success. It finds untapped market niches by spending time with its customers, looking for gaps. It listens. Back in the kitchen, the food scientists tinkered, concocting creations with fewer calories and ones with more iron, calcium, and folic acid.

Like so many breakthrough products, the Luna bar was

Clif's Luna Bar. *(© 2010 Clif Bar)*

initially panned by the experts. Ferguson recalls people in the industry discouraging the company from launching the product, arguing that it would cannibalize the flagship Clif Bar business. "We got people saying, if you do that, you're going to cut off half the market," Ferguson says. She remembers concerns from outsiders about Luna bars being too niche. "We got all the jokes from men. 'If I eat this bar, am I going to grow breasts?'"

But the company trusted its instincts. For the first year, it forecast sales of 1.5 million units. It sold 10 million. "We couldn't keep up with production," Ferguson says. What's more, the Clif Bar business kept growing without even a hiccup. "We always build a cannibalization factor into everything we do," Ferguson says. "But it's never black-and-white. If you get too scared about changing the past, you'll never innovate."

More than just a bar, Luna became a culture at Clif. It was the only energy-food company to focus specifically on women. And women noticed, rewarding the company with loyalty. Clif fosters that by sponsoring women-specific events, like LunaFest, a festival of short films by, for, and about women, and starting the Luna Moms Club, an online community to support new mothers. Georgia Gould, the Olympian on the Epiphany Ride, cycles for the Luna Chix Pro Team. It works because it's authentic. Clif doesn't just stop at listening to customers. It works hard to understand them. "The magic is when you hear all that [customer feedback] and it gels with what you have in your gut," Ferguson says. "There is great instinct here."

I mentioned that I'm a cyclist. The Clif product that resonates most for me came from the mind of Tom Richardson, a hard-core rock climber who once ranked third in the nation in sport climbing. He joined Clif in 1997, managing the company's Shot brand, the goolike gel that runners and cyclists squirt in their mouths for an instant carb injection. It was and remains an acquired taste. "Putting it in your mouth is such a strange sensation to a lot of people," Richardson says. Like me.

It was clear to Richardson that a significant portion of potential Shot customers were never going to use the product. The flavor is weird. The mouth-feel of the gel is odd. "I'm a tinkerer. I was thinking, how can we package Shots differently?" Richardson says. "It just sort of nagged at me for months." That nagging sensation sounds a bit like REI's David Mydans's obsession over the Quarter Dome tent, doesn't it? Just like Mydans, Richardson couldn't let it go. He kept tinkering.

That December, Richardson found himself in Peet's Coffee & Tea shop a few blocks from Clif headquarters.

138 As he stood in line to place his order, he watched customer after customer dip their hands into a bowl of Christmas cookie samples. Inspiration struck. "There was no hurdle for people," Richardson recalls. "They could reach their hand in and pop it into their mouth."

Next stop, the Mary Erickson Test Kitchen. Initially, Richardson wanted to create something like a big M&M, with a hard shell encasing the Shot goop. But some initial testing quickly showed the flaws of that approach. A few good bumps in shipping, and the shells cracked, letting the goop seep out. "From a durability standpoint, that didn't work," Richardson says.

So he tinkered some more. Design mavens would call it ideation. Richardson made the goop solid, like a gummy bear. "It was a natural progression," Richardson says. "We thought, let's just gel the gel." This way, the energy shots wouldn't leak in shipping. Next, Richardson and his crew had to figure out the right size for each block. One Shot offers a hundred calories, a precisely measured quantity for athletes to easily track their carb intake. But a hundred-calorie block would have been nearly baseball-size, too big to eat. So Clif settled on thirty-three-calorie marshmallow-size chunks, and dubbed them Shot Bloks. "Bloks are almost a piece of equipment," Richardson says. Athletes expect them to work precisely as advertised. If they don't live up to expectations, those athletes will know instantaneously, and they won't use the brand again.

Clif's Shot Bloks. (© 2010 Clif Bar)

Like Michael Mauer at Porsche and David Mydans at REI, Richardson never put Shot Bloks in front of a focus group. Instead, the company prototyped Bloks for a year, revising the product eight or ten times. It handed them out to Erickson and many others at the company—guys like Chris Randall, a competitive triathlete who manages the Shot brand. "The reason is, we are the consumer," Richardson explains. Clif trusts its instincts, because they are rooted in a deep understanding of what customers want. Even when it reaches out to customers for guidance—when it created the Luna bar, for example—it merely reaffirms the direction the company intends to go. "All of us saw early on that this was a great solution. We knew it in our guts," Richardson says. And they were right. "With Bloks, we nailed it right off the bat. They were so well received from the moment we launched them," Richardson says. "What I love about Bloks is that it is such a simple solution."

Of course, there was still room for improvement. Clif Shots are self-contained single-serving packages. Runners or cyclists simply pull one out, tear the top off with their teeth, and squeeze the goop into their mouths. "One thing we knew from the gel user is that it had to be opened with one hand and teeth," Richardson says. "We wanted to make sure it wasn't a two-handed operation."

Not so with the original Blok packaging. When they first hit the market, Bloks came in six-cube packs. It was easy to tear the packaging with your teeth, but you still had to stick a finger or two inside to fish around for a cube. "Our head just wasn't there yet," Richardson says. "We knew that we wanted to do better from a packaging standpoint."

One day, Ian Duffy, who works in Clif's manufacturing operations, visited the contract production facility a few hours south in Santa Cruz. As he and his counterpart at the firm walked through the "bone yards," the area set aside for idle equipment, Duffy, who once raced bikes professionally in Portugal, asked about a particular machine. "He was painfully aware that we needed a better package," Richardson says. Turns out the machine could package all six of the Bloks in a row, making it easy to squeeze from the end to deliver one cube at a time.

Product development at Clif may sound more seat-of-the-pants than it really is. There is a process. "It's getting more formalized," Richardson says. The company looks at category benchmarks and gold standards, trying to measure its development and manufacturing processes against others in the food industry. But don't think of Clif's design process as anything like the LEGO Innovation Model or OXO's design approach. At Clif, staffed with designers intimately familiar with the industry because they are the customers, instinct is never repressed. "The process is an avenue. But it doesn't restrict us," Richardson says.

It's a philosophy that Erickson baked into the company from the beginning, one he picked up during a bike trip to Europe in 1986 with his buddy Jay Thomas, the same guy who rode with Erickson on the original Epiphany Ride. The duo wanted to climb the famous alpine passes featured in the Tour de France and Giro d'Italia. They started in Lucerne, Switzerland, and, using a map Erickson brought along, made their way to Grosse Scheidegg in the Bernese Alps. The map showed one road, a thick red line, to take them there. Turns

141

out it was a highway. Cars and trucks buzzed by them. The pair eventually pulled off the road and found an alternate route to the pass.

As they traversed the Alps, they realized that they had the wrong map. It covered large swaths of Europe, and the roads were always those red ones—big, busy highways that offer the quickest route, but rarely the most fulfilling journey. So the pair bought a new map, one covered with white lines, less-traveled roads through fascinating villages. Every day with the new map was an adventure, full of risk—the road might peter out—and reward—spectacular vistas, local cuisine, interesting people.

From that, Erickson took a lesson that he uses to guide the business strategy at Clif to this day. Red-road companies, he says, are all about the destination—maximizing shareholder value. Shareholders expect those companies to grow at a certain rate. They might need to borrow money or take on new investors to meet those expectations. All those moves hand control over to others.

White-road companies, by contrast, set their own goals. They can experiment with new products and pace their development schedules. White-road companies don't have to answer to shareholders. They don't have to make quarterly numbers. They can't be irresponsible, but white-road companies have the freedom to take leaps of faith and trust their instincts. Clif Bar is, of course, a white-road company. "We go at our own pace," Erickson says. "We don't get a product out the door if it's not ready." Sounds more than a little bit like OXO's approach to its LiquiSeal Travel Mug.

Erickson knows a bit about being a red-road company

142

because Clif was one at one point. Erickson and his original partner, Lisa Thomas, were on the verge of selling the company in 2000 to Quaker for $120 million. But Erickson had second thoughts. On the day he was supposed to sign the papers, he decided to buy Thomas out instead. That meant taking on debt, and within an instant Erickson had became beholden. He had to answer to bankers.

Shortly after, the low-carb craze, fueled by the popularity of the Atkins and South Beach diets, was sweeping the country. Against his better instincts, Erickson was drawn in. Clif Bar, which had built its business pumping carbs into athletes, was getting pressure from bankers as well as retailers to jump on the bandwagon and make a quick buck in order to pay down debt. Erickson relented. Clif launched Luna Glow, bars that had as little as two carbohydrates compared to the original Luna bars, which have as many as twenty-nine carbs. And even though they came in flavors such as Strawberry Caramel Sundae and Fudge Almond Brownie, they sold poorly. "We created a very lousy, inauthentic product that wasn't Clif Bar. And it bombed," Erickson says. It was a me-too bar with nonorganic ingredients. Clif lost about $1 million on it.

In hindsight, it's clear to Erickson. There's no way for Clif Bar, a company defined by the energy foods it develops for athletes, to create an authentic low-carb bar. It would be like Porsche designing an economy car or REI selling formal wear. The company was following a trend rather than blazing a new trail. Its customers didn't want low-carb bars, and when the Atkins fad passed, new customers weren't interested, either. "Low-carb is an era in the company that is still

143

painful to me to this day," Erickson says. "We'll hopefully never do something like that again."

Both Erickson and his wife, Kit Crawford, who runs the company with him, are adamant about the importance of expecting and accepting failure. "We learn a ton from [failure]," Crawford says. At Clif, no one tries to sweep mistakes under the carpet. The low-carb debacle is discussed openly. "It's an opportunity to learn," Erickson says. "Everybody in the company knows the stories. It's part of the folklore." Just as at REI, OXO, and Nike.

Take Mojo bars—the sweet and savory bars that are more snack than energy food. They come in flavors such as Mixed Nuts and Peanut Butter Pretzel. The idea for Mojo came as Erickson was tinkering in his kitchen, inspired by a recent Thai meal. He baked a cookie sheet full of Thai peanut bars, saltier than regular Clif Bars, brought them to the annual company camping trip, and handed them out to employees. At Clif, employees are proxies for the company's customers. "I said, 'Try these and don't talk about it,'" he recalls.

Pretty quickly, Clif brought the savory bars to market. Sales were mixed. Within a year, Clif pulled the bars off the market and went back into the kitchen. The savory flavors were just a bit too extreme. Thai peanut was shelved. Instead, Clif stuck with more conventional flavors and relaunched Mojo in 2004. "We were probably ahead of our time," says Crawford. Mojo is now one of Clif's core products, growing at a nearly 50 percent clip in 2008.

144

It's one of the risks of trusting instinct and taking chances. Clif gets things right most of the time, but not always. The original Mojo bar was on the right track. The company just missed with its choices for flavors. But Erickson knew that his instincts weren't wrong. They were just a bit misguided. He looked at the failure as something of a prototype. And he learned from it, tweaking the original idea into something customers did want. And that's the lesson of Clif Bar: Develop a culture of authenticity and trust it to design products customers crave.

7

ACE HOTELS

The clock hasn't quite hit nine A.M. and midtown Manhattan is already pulsing to its brisk workday beat. The spring sun is out, the day is warming quickly, and I'm stepping lively to keep pace with the sea of workers streaming toward their offices. As I double-time it down Eighth Avenue for my nine-thirty meeting with Alex Calderwood, one of the travel industry's newest stars, I feel my mobile phone vibrate.

At thirty-nine, Calderwood is an unlikely hotel baron. His long black ringlets of hair fall with astonishing volume to his shoulders. When I met with him the afternoon before, he was wearing blue jeans and canvas high-top sneakers. His white button-down dress shirt sounds more formal than it actually looked.

Since 1999, the company Calderwood runs with three friends has opened three of the most talked about new hotels in the travel press. The first was the Ace Hotel Seattle, once a down-and-out maritime flophouse just north of downtown.

Calderwood and company spit-polished the place more than refurbished it. The hotel retains much of its well-worn charm, still sporting its original wood-plank floors and rough brick walls. It wasn't outfitted with new fixtures and furnishings; much of the decor was salvaged from spots such as a demolished nursing home and the old Boeing surplus outlet. That's one reason the rooms are a bargain, starting at seventy-five dollars a night for a minimalist flat with shared bathrooms down the hall.

Ace Hotel Seattle room. *(Courtesy of Ace Hotel)*

The simplicity of the Seattle spot resonated with travelers so much that eight years later, the group opened a second retro-chic hotel three hours south in Portland. In February 2009, Ace debuted its third hotel, this one with a bit of mid-century modern minimalism, in swank Palm Springs.

The nascent hotel chain has leaned heavily on design to distance itself from rivals and has won plaudits not just from the traditional travel press but also from design magazines such as *Monocle*, *I.D.*, *Wallpaper**, and *Dwell*. But the Ace experience isn't aimed at well-heeled travelers accustomed to valet service for their BMWs and instantaneous delivery of Dom Perignon by room service. Instead, Ace uses design to win over cost-conscious travelers, content with three-star accommodations but not with cookie-cutter chain-hotel mediocrity.

I first met Calderwood in the unfinished shell of Ace's most ambitious project yet—a 258-room hotel set to open just a few weeks later in one of the most competitive travel markets in the world—New York City. Like the other Ace hotels, the New York spot is eclectic, spare, and, even in its unfinished stage, already showing signs of being hip. That morning in New York, I'm heading back for the second round of conversations with Calderwood.

Except there's that matter of my ringing phone. Calderwood is on the other end, begging for my forgiveness. "I'm going to be honest with you," he says, his voice a bit scratchy and soft. "I was out really late last night and I just woke up." He's not feeling 100 percent, he tells me. I'm thinking he's probably approaching 50 percent. We need to reschedule for next Tuesday, when I'll be back in my Seattle home and

Calderwood comes west. Except that I will get an e-mail from his assistant that morning telling me of a "miscommunication" that led Calderwood to miss his flight. So we will reschedule to meet a week later in Seattle, and Calderwood will again have to cancel because of pressing business in New York.

Welcome to life at Ace Hotels. Calderwood is the front man for this ever-morphing enterprise, one that seems to thrive on the creative chaos of the moment. It's a company that reflects the genius, drive, and personality of Calderwood and his partners, and has flourished because of it. And he's adamant about heaping credit and praise on the others, in part because he's the one who often handles the press and gets the accolades. As a chaotic and often overscheduled group, they've come up with a vision for Ace Hotels—everything from the retro turntables in many of the rooms to the high-tech customized video-on-demand system featuring art-house flicks—that distinguishes the company from its bland, vanilla rivals, pricier spots such as Marriott hotels or discount chains such as Embassy Suites.

Of all the design-centric companies in this book, Ace is the smallest. It has the fewest employees and the least complex ownership structure. Its operating costs for a year are a fraction of the amount behemoths such as Porsche and Nike spend in just a few days. But Ace's model, because it relies so much on the insight and vision of just a handful of people and lacks much in the way of structure, may just be the most difficult to emulate.

What's more, in a few years, this chapter could read more like a cautionary tale than a shining example. The Ace model

152

may be difficult to replicate, but it's even harder to scale. The New York opening is the biggest project the company has ever taken on. To manage it, Calderwood moved to New York from his Seattle home. He struggles to schedule meetings more than a day in advance, and even when he does, as I learned this morning, he can't always make them. Ace is considering adding new locations, which is likely to stretch the already-thin Calderwood into translucence. He acknowledges this and says he and his partners are trying to figure out how to grow the company without losing the ethos it embodies. "But I don't have an answer for you," Calderwood says.

Still, there are some important lessons that the rolling funhouse that is Ace can offer. Perhaps the most important is that design is more than a way to make things expensive. Ace may be one of the best examples of how to use design to compete in the midmarket. After all, it isn't just wealthy folks who enjoy nicely made goods and well-thought-out services. Ace has built a business fixing up low-end dumps just enough to welcome creative types, and those they influence, but not so much as to make its rooms prohibitively expensive. "We take one- and two-star properties and get three- and four-star rates," Calderwood says.

The roots of the company stretch back to Seattle in the early 1990s, when Calderwood joined his friend Wade Weigel to launch Rudy's Barbershop, a place where tattooed and pierced hair cutters will give you a ten-dollar buzz cut or a twenty-one-dollar style in an old-fashioned barber chair. Rudy's found fans in Seattle's alternative rock music scene in part by selling concert tickets and CDs—Calderwood ran a show promotion company at the time called Tasty Shows.

153

It built a following with the city's young art scene by doing things like commissioning a mural by Shepard Fairey, who gained his greatest recognition years later for his iconic Barack Obama "HOPE" poster during the 2008 presidential campaign. The group took out no loans, funding the company from savings and plowing profits into opening new shops in the chain, which now has more than a dozen locations in Seattle, Portland, and Los Angeles.

The group realized they'd stumbled upon something of a formula, a way to use design to tap into a young, hip demographic that marketers take such pains to reach. Weigel and other friends opened a variety of restaurants and bars in Seattle, each on a bit of shoestring, with a dose of funky used furniture, original creations from local artists, and a price that wouldn't keep low-wage twentysomethings away. And they found that the price and the vibe attracted a creative niche of thirty- and fortysomethings too.

Though neither Calderwood nor Weigel had ever run a hotel, the pair thought the formula might work there as well. Seattle had plenty of high-end hotels at its core and a handful of lower-cost, generic chains ringing the outskirts of downtown. What it didn't have was the kind of European hotel that the two entrepreneurs had visited when they traveled abroad—hip, hostel-like spots. They wanted the sort of place where visitors could get a bargain by using a shared bathroom down the hall, with a common area where they would want to gather and meet fellow travelers. "We wanted something different, like an artist's loft," Weigel says. They spent months brainstorming ideas, long before they ever had a hotel where they could try them out.

One of Weigel's business associates mentioned a funky property he had recently acquired just north of downtown Seattle, in a gentrifying neighborhood known as Belltown. He wondered if Weigel had any ideas for the place. The building wasn't much. It had been a halfway house most recently, and years before was a maritime flophouse for Seattle's booming fishing industry. But Weigel and Calderwood saw the potential. They created storyboards for the hotel, collecting photos of people and objects that evoked the kind of feeling they wanted for the place. It gave them a touchstone to refer back to that made every aspect of the hotel feel cohesive.

With a limited budget, the pair kept costs low by shopping for furniture and fixtures at consignment shops and surplus outlets. Instead of remodeling the whole place, Weigel and Calderwood left most elements intact. That means that half of the twenty-eight rooms have bathrooms, and the other half share a handful of huge, clean showers and toilets down the hall. The beds in the rooms are custom-built low-slung platforms, which tend to give each room an airier feel. The pair opened the Seattle hotel in 1999 and invited a friend, Doug Herrick, who was working as a landscape architect at the time, to run it. (Herrick has since become a partner.)

More than a decade later, the place still feels hip. The rooms are cozy without feeling small, warm without feeling stuffy. The blankets are wool, the stainless-steel sinks feel like they belong in a restaurant, and the chairs and sofas—all purchased from consignment stores, vintage furniture shops, and garage sales—are the kind you want to flop into. The hotel

155

includes fun touches, like mirrors with "You are beautiful" etched at the bottom and paintings by pop artists such as KAWS (the same guy who designs shoes for Nike).

Ace Hotel rooms evoke the kind of apartment you might have had right after college. Or at least, the apartment you wish you had. This isn't Design Within Reach furniture, sumptuous Italian leather sofas with warm blond-wood cabinets and soft Scandinavian duvets. The Ace is all about functional design.

This approach kept costs down and meant that Ace could charge well below established four-star-hotel rates in Seattle, even though the hip vibe still attracts some of the crowd that might have opted for plusher digs. Deluxe rooms, the ones with bathrooms, go for $195 a night. At the same time, Ace is pulling in younger travelers with rooms as low as $75, for those willing to trudge down the hall to use the bathroom. And those younger travelers help keep the hip vibe going and make the place more appealing to the affluent customers.

The first time I stay at an Ace, it's the Portland location. It's easy to see how the idea behind Ace has evolved over time. The flat light from a gray March morning streams through four gloriously large windows in room 300 at the former Clyde Hotel, another run-down property that Ace spiffed up. At most hotels, particularly budget ones like the Ace, room 300 isn't much different from 301, 422, or 109. Maybe the bathroom is on the left as you walk in the door instead of the right. Perhaps the artwork features prints of lilacs and daisies rather than roses and tulips.

But, as in Seattle, every room at the Portland Ace is different. Each is furnished largely with items found just about anywhere but in a hotel furnishings catalog. The desk in room 300 is a plank of wood about eight feet long and two feet wide. Ace reclaimed the timber when it refurbished the hotel, originally built in 1912. One end of the plank is bolted to the wall and the other is held up by a chest of drab-green army-issue drawers.

My bed is a king-size mattress on top of a one-foot-high wood stand. The nightstands on either side are blocks of wood. The bathroom, behind sliding wood doors, features a claw-foot tub with hot- and cold-water spigots similar to the one in my grandparents' house decades ago. Clamp lamps, ordinary silver lights that look like oversize camera flashbulbs, light the room. And while my room has no art on the walls, other rooms at the hotel that I've had a chance to peek into feature murals by local Portland artists such as Brent Wick, who painted, among other things, a giant cat. Eleven of the eighty-nine rooms don't have a bathroom. And three of those rooms have bunk beds, favored by visiting families as a place for older kids who can traipse down the hall to their parents' room when they need to use the bathroom. The rates run from $85 to $250 a night.

The hotel isn't so basic that there aren't any creature comforts. The glass-doored minifridge sits ready to chill a bottle of wine or beer. And there's a huge Sony flat-panel television with all the cable stations you could want. But just so the hotel doesn't get too far from its funky vibe, every room also comes with a working turntable and a selection of vinyl records. Room 300 includes *The Heart-Touching Magic of Jim Nabors*, *Head Games* by Foreigner, and the original soundtrack to *Last Tango in Paris*. There's also a photo

157

Ace Hotel Portland bunk-bed room. *(Photo by John Mark Sorum. Courtesy of Ace Hotel)*

booth in the lobby, a guest favorite that Ace has subsequently included in its Palm Springs and New York locations.

When Calderwood and I eventually connect again, more than a month has passed since our aborted meeting, and we're baking in the 102-degree heat of Palm Springs, California. This is the first of the properties to target resort travelers. It has two pools and a spa, but still aims for a hippie, desert vibe. So rather than cool off by the pool, Calderwood, Herrick, and hotel manager Jonathan Heath are scouring local consignment shops and used-furniture stores for a few pieces to add a bit more character to the place. At the moment, Calderwood is obsessed with macramé. He'd love a huge

158

piece to hang in The Commune, the event center at the hotel. Heath, though, has stumbled on something else that catches his fancy.

"There's a pretty cool coyote out there," he tells Calderwood at a consignment store where a handful of gems nestle amid the second-rate chaises, dining tables, and sofas. Much of the bric-a-brac, Calderwood guesses, are the former belongings of the recently deceased in this enclave disproportionately populated with retirees.

"Oh, my god, that's really great," Calderwood enthuses upon seeing the stuffed but still slightly cheerful coyote perched on a piece of wood. He looks at the price tag—$350. "That's

Ace Hotel Palm Springs room. *(Photo by Douglas Lyle Thompson and Jon Johnson. Courtesy of Ace Hotel)*

159

really cheap for taxidermy," he says, the voice of a man who's clearly purchased a few dead animals in his time. The three debate whether to put the coyote in the bar, the restaurant, or the lobby before Herrick encourages the others to hold off on the purchase. The budget is limited and macramé is the order of the day. "I'm the voice of reason," Herrick says.

So much of Ace's ethos is captured in the tiniest of touches. The coyote evokes a twenty-foot-long diorama above the Palm Springs reception desk that features another coyote, this one baring its teeth, set in the Palm Springs desert, with quail, a prairie dog, some California cactus, and the San Jacinto Mountains in the background. But harried travelers, eager to find their rooms, unpack their bags, and dive into the pool, could be forgiven for not even noticing the piece as they check in.

While the Palm Springs hotel is a resort, it still has much of the rough-hewn feel that's come to be Ace's signature. "We like things a little imperfect," Calderwood says. When the company refurbished the place—once a Howard Johnson's motel that had sat unused for years—it ripped out the carpeting in the rooms and never replaced it. Left behind are concrete slabs with cracks that spider out randomly, with the barest of coverings from southwestern-style throw rugs. The curtains and bedspreads are canvas painter's tarps, and bathroom hooks are made from the elbows of plumbing pipes.

But Ace is beginning to add a bit more polish to its properties, starting with Palm Springs. In addition to the pools and spa, it has a twenty-four-hour gym. There are three cozy yurts—funky, no doubt—near the pool where guests can receive massages.

160

Even the rooms are a bit spiffier. While Ace purchased more than a thousand vintage items for the hotel, much of the furniture, though still basic, is new, such as the blond-wood footlockers used to stash extra pillows. It's not the army surplus gear you'll find in Portland. The desks in the rooms are spartan, to be sure—just a long top with fold-up legs. But they, too, were purchased new. That's the price of opening a 180-room hotel, a size that is much harder to equip on a tight timeline with individually purchased furnishings from flea markets and the like.

The sheen isn't lost on Calderwood, and it makes him a bit uncomfortable. "We worked differently than we worked before," he says. The company picked up a few more items from catalogs. The place still has the hip Ace vibe, but it's just a bit more refined, a bit less imperfect. It's one reason why Calderwood is looking for macramé, a high-profile used item that will make the place seem more worn, like the life-size macramé elephant head in the restaurant. "Now is the time to scuff up the place a little bit," Calderwood says.

It was even harder to keep that homemade feel at the 258-room New York hotel. Ace took over the Hotel Breslin, a building that opened in 1904 and sits in a tourist no-man's-land south of the Empire State Building. When it came time to furnish the place, Ace couldn't just shop randomly at used-furniture stores. There are just too many rooms.

So Calderwood headed to Massachusetts for the Brimfield Antiques Show, one of the biggest flea markets in the country. He took along Robin Standefer and Stephen Alesch of the New York design firm Roman & Williams, who helped create the Ace New York and has done interior design for celebrities

161

such as Ben Stiller, Gwyneth Paltrow, and Kate Hudson. There, they grabbed chairs, lamps, and tables, including an eighteen-foot laboratory work surface with a giant slate top that's now part of the public workspace in the hotel.

Because so much was needed, Ace also worked with Roman & Williams to create pieces that fit the feel of the hotel. That meant designing tables with knotty B-grade plywood, something that baffled contract manufacturers. "They

Ace Hotel Palm Springs, poolside. *(Photo by Douglas Lyle Thompson and Jon Johnson. Courtesy of Ace Hotel)*

thought they'd get fired," Standefer says. They used plumbing pipe as hang bars, saving space normally taken up by closets. And the modest bathrooms led them to install beefy canvas sheets with pockets to stash toiletries, rolled-up hand towels, and the like next to the sinks. "The budget served the aesthetic of the property really well," Alesch says.

If all of this just sounds like something that's merely cool and not great business, think again. Those design decisions

have led to huge cost savings. In the hotel business, bean counters keep their eyes on FF&E—furniture, fixtures, and equipment—one of the benchmark expenses in hotel construction. In New York, FF&E for a nice three- or four-star hotel can run as high as $40,000 per room and is typically in the $25,000 range, according to Jonathan Sebbane, vice president at hospitality industry consultant HVS. Ace pulled off the remodel of the old Breslin for $15,000 a room. That means Ace can charge less for rooms there than can rivals at the plusher hotels and siphon off some business.

And that's what happened. Shortly after opening, the New York Ace inked corporate deals with the likes of Walmart and mammoth corporate law firm Skadden, Arps, Slate, Meagher & Flom, each of which get a discounted rate for agreeing to book a certain number of rooms in a year. "It's not just hipsters who are interested," says Andrew Zobler, the chief executive of GFI Development, which owns the hotels in both New York and Palm Springs and contracted with Ace to design and run them. "It's a wider audience who appreciate the value proposition."

Ace has also learned that design isn't just good for bringing guests in; the company can also use it to boost ancillary sales. In Palm Springs, for example, Ace commissioned Evan Hecox, an illustrator for Chocolate Skateboards, to create illustrations inspired by California desert scenes. Ace turned those illustrations into posters, and hung a few in each room by binder clips from the wood-slatted walls. Guests can buy them right off the wall for $125 to $175, just by checking a box on the minibar menu. And the canvas bathroom caddy in the New York hotel is a nifty enough creation that guests

164

have been asking where to find them to use at home. So Ace is planning to sell those too at the front desk, although it hasn't fixed a price yet.

The design vibe sounds almost formulaic. But it's not, and that's what makes it so hard to replicate. Often, the partners and the various design firms they've hired will brainstorm for hours. They'll jot down words that evoke the feel they're trying to achieve at a particular property. They'll dig out photos that capture the vibe. And they'll put them all on storyboards, big posters that they can refer back to as they put together a hotel. And often their best ideas come while shopping together at Brimfield or a local consignment shop.

Perhaps the key to Ace's success is its willingness to take risks. Indeed, the company seeks them out. Most big hotels would shoot down the idea of putting turntables in rooms, for example, worried that needles would break or records would be stolen. But Calderwood thought it could be a fun way to differentiate. "My gut instinct is that it'd be a signature moment," Calderwood says. "Let's not live in fear. This is not going to be a huge financial exposure." The turntables are so popular in Portland that guests make sure they get a room with one. That's why Ace put some in rooms in Palm Springs and New York as well.

Of course, the company is not immune to making mistakes. In New York, Ace wanted more table space in rooms where guests could plunk down bags. It found a funky old folding table that it wanted to replicate, and hired a contract builder to create dozens of them. But when the first one came back, it looked contrived. "We tried to mimic the

165

idea," Calderwood said. "It wasn't authentic." So Ace hired a local craftsman and gave him space in the hotel basement to create a shop to build the tables individually, instead of mass-producing them. He took salvaged wood and attached industrial legs to each piece. They were exactly what Calderwood wanted, each one a little imperfect, a little different.

Perhaps Ace's biggest risk these days is managing its growth. The privately held company has never posted a losing year, Calderwood says. In the year before the Palm Springs and New York openings, Ace rang up $4.5 million in annual sales, growing 10 percent. The new openings should roughly quintuple that take. And Ace expects sales to jump another 50 percent again in 2010. That success is generating calls from hotel property owners around the country and in other spots worldwide to see if Ace will design and run their new locations. Ace, though, is still struggling to manage its existing business. "We're definitely having some growing pains right now," Herrick says. When we talked in the spring of 2009, the partners were discussing hiring a head of finance and a head of operations to take on some of the less creative tasks the partners handle. Though by early 2010, it hadn't hired anyone for the job. Until that happens, GFI chief executive Zobler has made sure that his staff remains very hands-on with regard to Ace's operations, both to protect the business and to educate the young company.

Beyond creating a structure to handle its size, the Ace partners have to figure out how to make sure the design ethos of the brand doesn't get watered down as it expands. They'd all like to add another half-dozen or so hotels over the next few years. "We know that it's one hotel at a time," Weigel

166

Ace Hotel New York room. *Art by Andrew Pork. (Photo by Douglas Lyle Thompson and Jon Johnson. Courtesy of Ace Hotel)*

says. "It's the only way to do what we do." But at that slower pace, the partners can't run the existing properties and add so many new ones by themselves. That means hiring creative staff and entrusting them with carrying the Ace brand forward. Calderwood acknowledges the challenge, even if he hasn't quite addressed it yet. "We will have to design a paradigm that will evolve with us," Calderwood says.

What's generating so much interest, ironically, is that Ace isn't trying to create an experience that appeals to the broadest possible demographic. It's the very opposite of OXO's Universal Design strategy. My octogenarian dad and septuagenarian mom would probably struggle getting into beds slung so low. Starched shirts might have a hard time finding a conference room for a meeting. And social conservatives

167

might blanch at all the tattoos on the staff and many of the customers.

That's just fine with Ace. It's not trying to create a bland experience that is palatable for everyone but loved by no one. "We designed a place where we wanted to stay," Herrick says, sitting in a chair from a shuttered bowling alley in the breakfast room at the Seattle Ace. Just like Ferry Porsche, Lloyd Anderson, and Gary Erickson, the Ace guys created their business for themselves. Herrick and his partners developed a brand that they are passionate about, believing that would be enough to fuel the same enthusiasm among customers. So far, it's worked.

8

VIRGIN ATLANTIC

London has just been slammed with the worst winter storm it's had in a generation. Sleet and snow blanket the city, as deep as a foot in some spots, clogging roads and disrupting trains and buses. Drivers are being told to travel only if necessary, keeping many workers home. The situation is so dire that the London Ambulance Service is saying it will respond only to calls deemed "life threatening." The city is paralyzed.

It would be hard to find a place where this is more obvious than Heathrow Airport. London's biggest airport is limiting flights to just one runway. Over two days, nearly one thousand flights have been canceled. The conditions are so dicey that one flight, a Cyprus Airways jet, skidded off the runway on landing. Luckily, no one was hurt.

171

In the terminal, passengers are on edge. Many have missed flights, missed connections, missed opportunities to visit family or spend time on vacation, skiing where it's supposed to snow or sunning somewhere much, much warmer. Some travelers are curled up on the terminal floor, waiting—hoping—to be on a flight somewhere soon.

I'm at Heathrow too. But my biggest concern right now is how I want Lizzy to trim my hair. She's the stylist in the Virgin Atlantic Clubhouse, the swinging airport lounge for Virgin's Upper Class customers. I dropped $2,790.84 to fly Virgin to Europe, and most of that went toward my first-class—Virgin calls it Upper Class—ticket from Heathrow

Virgin Atlantic Clubhouse hair salon, Heathrow Airport.
(Courtesy of Virgin Atlantic)

172

back to Newark, New Jersey. I wanted to get a taste of how Virgin has used design to create an experience that has built a loyal following among customers.

For me, that experience starts with Lizzy suggesting I keep the top a little longer than the sides. She's too polite to say so, but what she really means is that the length gives me a wee bit more volume to mask that annoyingly increasing shine from the center of my scalp, where hair used to be. Like all the hairstylists in the Clubhouse, Lizzy was trained at the swanky New York salon Bumble and bumble. So I leave myself to Lizzy's devices and pretty soon I'm coifed, shampooed, and ready for a bite to eat.

That's my next dilemma. I'm trying to eat healthy, so I start with a delicious Niçoise salad from the deli. But that snack turns into a hankering for a full meal. And because it's approaching six P.M., I opt for the vegetable jalfrezi, something of an Indian stir-fry that comes with naan and basmati rice. I enjoy the rich and complex flavors while listening to Welsh pop star Duffy singing her song "Enough Love," yearning for more of that precious emotion, in the background. My thoughts turn to the plain airport food, and the cacophony of airport announcements, rolling luggage carts, and crying babies assaulting the poor stranded traveler outside the blissful confines of the Clubhouse. But only briefly.

You might argue that I was just living large, the way anyone traveling first class does. And you wouldn't be entirely wrong. No doubt the neighboring lounges of Cathay Pacific Airways and Singapore Airlines offered tasty food and plush services. It's hard to make a case that Virgin Atlantic is a bleeding-edge innovator, either. It got into the airline

173

business late. It uses the same jets, flies the same routes, and lives by the same strict safety regulations that restrict much of its ability to differentiate.

And yet it does. Virgin has figured out how to use design—both industrial and service design—to create an experience that breeds loyalty among its customers. It's created some of the most comfortable seats in the aviation world. Its Clubhouses throw off a good-time vibe that's part Austin Powers, part James Bond. And its in-flight service is inevitably cheerful, cheeky, and even glamorous.

Think about that for second. When was the last time you really looked forward to getting on an airplane? When was the last time you told a friend about a great experience you had flying somewhere? These days, air travel is little more than a glorified bus ride. Airlines, which have cut costs to save money, stuff as many passengers as possible into a long, metal tube. They serve up the blandest meals possible, designed to meet with the least resistance. Overworked flight attendants, dressed in authoritarian faux-military uniforms, often revert to a dictatorial style in an effort to control the masses. Passengers are forced to shell out money for things that were once considered fundamental airline services, such as checked luggage and even pillows. Passengers don't look forward to flying; they look forward to the ordeal being over.

Virgin Atlantic was born from that sort of frustration. The company's iconic leader, Sir Richard Branson, had been running the Virgin record label for several years, and traveling the globe in the process. Like just about every frequent flier, he loathed air travel. In the early 1980s, American Airlines canceled his flight from the Virgin Islands to Puerto Rico.

174

Fed up, Branson called a charter company and arranged to get a plane to fly the route for two thousand dollars. Then he divided the two thousand dollars it cost to charter the plane by the number of folks left stranded, jotted the number down on a borrowed blackboard, and walked through the terminal selling tickets for thirty-nine dollars a pop. He recalls "jokingly" writing "Virgin Airlines" on the blackboard. Like the genesis of so many great business ideas, Virgin Atlantic came from a simple revelation. "I thought there must be a better way," Branson recalls. Branson and I connect by phone while he's in New York for the twenty-fifth anniversary of the first Virgin Atlantic flight, and he's nostalgic.

Branson wanted travel to be fun, even glamorous, again. "We decided to create the kind of airline that myself and my friends would like to fly on," Branson says. There it is again, that idea of designing a business to meet the needs of the founder because nothing else like it existed. In catering to his own needs, Branson realized he'd address the unspoken desires of other travelers. That's what Ferry Porsche, Gary Erickson, and Alex Calderwood did. When Branson did it, airline industry pundits wondered what business someone from the entertainment industry had running an airline. "But that was exactly the point. The airline bosses had forgotten that people like to be entertained," Branson says.

Even in those early days, Branson focused on designing an experience that kept customers coming back. "If you design a home or a flat, you worry about the mood lighting," Branson says. "You worry about the quality of the carpets. You worry about the quality of the seats. You worry about the kind of crockery you're going to have. You make

175

sure people are entertained and that they have a good time. The same should apply to an airline. It should be a pleasant experience." He doesn't use the phrase "service design." But that's what Branson has mastered. And as the Western world has evolved into a service economy, it's a skill that continues to set the company apart. When the first Virgin Atlantic plane left London's Gatwick Airport for Newark in 1984, it had the first bar in business class. Its flight attendants wore stylish ruby-red uniforms that harkened back to a time when passengers looked forward to getting on an airplane.

I have that feeling as I settle into seat 3K on my Heathrow-to-Newark flight. My feet are resting comfortably on an ottoman, my legs fully extended. The window is on my right. All that's next to me on the left is the aisle, then a series of seats, similarly angled in a herringbone pattern throughout the Upper Class cabin. Virgin Atlantic pioneered the unusual configuration for its innovative Upper Class section. With those seats, passengers can get up, press a button, and watch the back of the seat flip down and become a lie-flat bed. Much nicer than the fully-reclined-but-still-slightly-angled seats offered in first class by some rivals.

Actually, Virgin Atlantic didn't have the first lie-flat bed. That breakthrough came from its archrival, British Airways. "It didn't sit well with us that our competitors could have a truly flat seat and we couldn't," says Joe Ferry, Virgin Atlantic's head of design. When I meet with Ferry, it's in a conference room at Virgin Atlantic's headquarters in Crawley, in the shadow of London's other major airport, Gatwick. He's wearing a pink button-down shirt with an open collar under a neatly tailored gray suit. His thinning salt-and-pepper hair

176

and short sideburns frame his angular face and easy smile. Ferry, who studied industrial design engineering at London's Royal College of Art, describes himself as "obsessed by seating through the ages." And for the record, he's sitting in the Series 7 chair designed by legendary Danish designer Arne Jacobsen.

Ferry's obsession led him to reconsider airline seating. But he had to do so in the midst of one of the most challenging economic periods in airline history. He began the design process mere months before terrorists turned hijacked planes into missiles on September 11, 2001. Air travel came to a virtual standstill. "The bottom had completely fallen out of the market," Ferry recalls. "We were hemorrhaging money."

Many companies buckle down in these conditions, keeping investments to a minimum until fortunes change. But history repeatedly shows that the companies who become more aggressive in lean markets are often the ones who jump ahead when the economy improves. And Virgin is nothing if not daring. "At no point did [the company's top executives] say we have to stop this project," Ferry says. "In fact, they said we have to ramp it up." To Branson, it's basic business theory: "In difficult times, you've got to stand head and shoulders above everyone else."

The airline didn't want to reduce the number of Upper Class seats, but it struggled to come up with a configuration that let passengers get truly horizontal. As they recline, ordinary airline seats either hit the passengers behind them or bump into the wall of the cabin. The "eureka moment," as Ferry describes it, came when he realized that if travelers got out of their seats and pressed a button that would flip

177

the back of the seat forward, flush with an ottoman, they could lie flat while at the same time conserving precious cabin space. Working with British design firm PearsonLloyd, Virgin Atlantic went from business case to prototype to launch in seventeen months.

Still, it was hardly a given that first-class passengers would be willing to unbuckle, stand up, press a button, wait about five seconds for the seat to become a bed, then hop back in, particularly when rival airlines weren't requiring their top-paying customers to do so. The payoff, though, is a bed that's eighty-two inches long and thirty-three inches wide in the upper deck of a Boeing 747-400, making it one of the biggest fully flat beds in the business. And because each side has a different purpose, Virgin was able to use different materials—a nice soft leather for the sitting side and a breathable fabric for the sleeping side.

Those seats, the centerpiece of a $115 million redesign of Virgin Atlantic's Upper Class in 2003, changed the dynamics of Virgin's business. "As soon as we rolled it out," Ferry says, "we knew it was going to be a critical success." Customer satisfaction soared. "There was massive daylight between us and competitors." The seat won awards from the Design Business Association in the United Kingdom and from design magazines such as *Wallpaper** and *I.D.* And most important, Virgin Atlantic saw a demonstrable market share shift, upward of 10 percent, among lucrative first-class passengers on long-haul routes.

178   We're barely airborne on my flight to Newark before the man in 2K flips his seat down to a bed. He's tucked in snugly, with a comfy duvet covering his body and his head

Virgin Atlantic Upper Class Suite seat. *(Courtesy of Virgin Atlantic)*

on a full-size pillow. An hour or so later, I'm catching some shut-eye as well.

As a traveler who can count the number of times he's flown first class on one hand, it's hardly surprising how much I love it. My every need is catered to. Charley, the eager-to-please flight attendant, brings over a glass of champagne to begin the journey. She hands me my Virgin Atlantic sleep kit, a set of pajamas to slip into as the evening wears on. Remembering to stay true to my diet, I tell Charley that I'll pass on both dessert selections, a tempting offering of either dark and white chocolate bread-and-butter pudding or a lemon posset. Graciously, she concocts an altogether too large selection of fresh fruit from the plane's stores.

Virgin Atlantic is never short on whimsy. Air travel comes with a nod and a wink because Virgin Atlantic believes that it can differentiate itself with its sense of humor. Consider the cheese knife, a dull spreading utensil that's all of five inches, sitting next to my plate. It has the words "Virgin Atlantic. FINEST STAINLESS STEAL" etched into it. That last word is a typo. Passengers swiped Virgin Atlantic's knives so frequently, the airline decided to run with it and encourage the petty theft, figuring the marketing benefit would outweigh the negligible cost. Now customers, like me, pocket the cutlery and share the story with others. "Humor is another important element of design," Branson says.

As Ferry describes designing that experience, he uses a metaphor I hadn't expected. "It's almost like creating a theater set," he explains. "It's creating props for our cast, our cabin crew." The props are the knives, the pajamas, the meal. The set includes everything from the lie-flat seat to the full walk-up bar, and goes down to more subtle touches like Swarovski crystal panels at the front of the cabin.

"If you draw the analogy of putting on a theater show," Ferry says, taking the metaphor further, "lighting is essential." The airline has a setting for boarding that's bright, but not too harsh. Another setting, intended to evoke candlelight, creates the appropriate ambiance for dining. There are fourteen settings in all, and each one fades into the next, never jolting passengers with the sudden burst of fluorescent brightness familiar to passengers on other airlines at the end of every flight. Mood lighting, fully-reclining seats, the good-time vibe of its Clubhouse lounge. All those things individually might seem like mere touches to make things just a bit more pleasant. But collectively, they are the heart of experience design that sets Virgin Atlantic apart from its rivals.

This luxury and attention to detail is well and good for the fine people who travel first class. But what about the rest of us in the back of the plane, where mildly unpleasant is often the best we can hope for? Virgin has used the lessons learned from its Upper Class service and applied them to its own economy class, as well as to a handful of smaller regional carriers it has launched around the globe.

One of its most daring efforts came in August 2007, when it debuted Virgin America, a cut-rate carrier created to compete with the likes of Southwest Airlines and Alaska Airlines with routes primarily along the West Coast. Starting a new airline is challenging enough, but Virgin did it just months before one of the worst economic cycles in aviation history, hammered by the double whammy of a sputtering economy and soaring fuel costs.

The company saw an opportunity, created by the lack of imagination demonstrated by the domestic U.S. carriers. "The American airline industry was absolutely awful," Branson says. "The consumer experience was dreadful and it's strange because in every other industry in America—restaurants and clubs and hotels—you've got people who've created wonderful designs, wonderful innovations. But when

181

it came to the air above the United States, it was pretty non-existent and it left Virgin America open to create an airline that is miles better than the rest."

Regulations prevent Virgin, or any foreign company, from owning a majority stake in a domestic carrier in the United States. So Virgin created a complex ownership structure that gives it less than 25 percent of voting stock in the company. That said, it's hard to think of Virgin America as anything but the offspring of Virgin Atlantic, even if it is competing as a discount carrier.

Start with its design pedigree. The executive who crafted the new airline's look and feel is Adam Wells, who worked for Ferry for four years before becoming design director at Virgin America. He's since moved on to become design director for New York–based Virgin USA, where he's looking into new American markets to inject the brand, including the hotel industry.

Wells brought much of the daring design ethos from Virgin Atlantic to the Burlingame, California, headquarters of Virgin America, despite the tighter budget. For instance, he wanted to re-create the elegant lighting system in Virgin Atlantic's Upper Class cabin. But pinching pennies meant making do without the same high-end LED lights. Using just fluorescent bulbs, Wells was able to design a system offering twelve different styles that flight attendants can adapt based on outside lighting. What's more, the windows have a slight blue tint to soften the light that streams in through them.

182   Because it operated with a start-up budget, Virgin America had few resources to prototype the lighting, or much else, as it designed its fleet. It relied heavily on suppliers, such as

Airbus Industrie, to prototype for it. Wells traveled frequently to the Airbus factories in Toulouse, France, to test his ideas. "I knew I was going to avoid yellow and green because it makes people nauseous," Wells says. But an early version of the lighting, for example, skewed too much in the other direction, toward pink. "People were saying it felt a little too much like a disco," Wells recalls. "They were asking, 'Where's the glitter ball?'" The airline toned that down before its debut.

Virgin America is as cheeky as its big cousin. Take the in-flight safety video. Instead of the typically stale and self-important live-action production, it's a cartoon, clever enough to hold your attention even if you've seen dozens of airplane safety videos before. As the narrator begins the message on a flight from Seattle to San Francisco four months after my London-to-Newark journey, I look around the plane. Most passengers' eyes seem to be focused on the nine-inch monitors on the seat backs in front of them, not at newspapers or books or even the backs of their eyelids, as you might expect on this seven A.M. flight.

They can't be learning anything new. The video, after all, covers the same material travelers have heard countless times before. But this video, like so many of Virgin's creations, is playful. When it instructs travelers to put away electronics, it shows a nun quickly disassembling and packing up her video-game paraphernalia. And it mocks the outdated notion of helping folks buckle their seat belts. "For the point zero zero zero one percent of you who have never operated a seat belt before, it works like this," the narrator says as the film shows a self-conscious matador proudly mastering the task only to have the bull sitting next to him roll his eyes dismissively.

183

Virgin America also shows how design can help generate a bit more cash and save the company a bit more in costs. It has created food service that challenges the conventions of the airline industry. For years, carriers offered free meals that were so consistently bad that they became a staple punch line for comedians. Some airlines have tried to change that business model, charging travelers. But there's often little choice and those meals generally don't taste much better.

Virgin America too decided that free wasn't necessarily better, and charges for its food. But it offers a selection that, while it may not be gourmet, is often pretty darn good and even healthy. On flights longer than two hours, passengers can choose from eight different entrees, including a Napa Valley Chicken Salad Hand Roll and a Spring Spinach Salad. My evening flight back from San Francisco is less than two hours, which means no full meals. But I pick up Hippie Chips' Haight-Ashberry Jalapeño chips for three dollars. The airline has even gotten creative with its drinks menu, becoming the first airline to offer absinthe, the anise-flavored spirit once banned in the United States for its reputed psychoactive properties. I give the eight-dollar liquor a try, mixing it with CranApple juice, and suffer no noticeable side effects.

Virgin America has even rethought the way it delivers its food, designing a more traveler-friendly approach. Flight attendants don't come around with an aisle-clogging cart at one time during the flight whether you're hungry or not. Instead, passengers order items from the touch-screen monitor on the seat back in front of them, paying with a credit card. Flight attendants deliver the food a few minutes later. Not only is it a better experience, it automates the food

184

service, keeping cash out of flight attendants' hands and improving inventory controls so that Virgin knows what to restock before the plane even lands.

Virgin America even rethought the barrier between first class and coach, creating a new revenue opportunity. On most airlines, that barrier is a thick panel, usually covered with drab wallpaper. It's not just unattractive, it's claustrophobic. It's even worse for the folks sitting behind the barrier, with their tray tables stuffed into their armrests. That makes the armrests wider, meaning there's less room for the already narrow seats. "We saw that as an opportunity to have a better row," Wells says.

Virgin America redesigned the barrier. The top half is made from a purple translucent material. The translucence

Virgin America Main Cabin Select seats. *(Courtesy of Virgin America)*

185

makes the space feel more open. The bottom half of the barrier includes a pull-out tray table, which means the seats can be the same size as the others in coach. And there's more leg room and no reclining seats in front to cut into that precious space. So Virgin America brands those seats, along with the more capacious exit-row spots, as Main Cabin Select, charging as much as twice the price of other seats in the cabin.

Every one of those design decisions requires a bit more effort, a bit more planning, and often a bit more initial cost. But there's a clear long-term payoff. "It restrains us from becoming a commodity," says David Cush, Virgin America's chief executive, who joined the company from American Airlines, where he climbed the corporate ladder through the finance ranks. Like its older sibling, Virgin America's customer-satisfaction data soar above those of rivals. The carrier won *Condé Nast Traveler*'s 2008 and 2009 Readers' Choice Awards for best domestic carrier.

By one financial benchmark for the industry, Virgin America is already on par with more established rivals Southwest Airlines and JetBlue Airways, earning about nine cents of revenue per available seat mile. Even though the airline is a discount carrier, Cush says he expects it to hit 90 to 95 percent of the twelve-cent industry average by 2012. "When I got here, I was skeptical of the value of design, to be honest," Cush says. "I've been convinced."

The Virgin brand is sometimes dismissed as being "all marketing." And there's little doubt that, like Nike, Virgin shines at promoting itself, its products, and its services. Much of that starts with Branson, among the world's most iconic executives. There are few more willing to go to the lengths Sir Richard does—piloting a hot-air balloon across the Atlantic Ocean to promote Virgin Atlantic, driving a tank down New York's Fifth Avenue to launch Virgin Cola in the United States, wearing a wedding gown to promote his Virgin Brides bridal-wear business.

"If you create a product that is a good product," Branson says, "it will not succeed, even if it's the best, unless you get out there and tell people about it and market it." Remember Nike's initial problems with its skateboard shoes marketing— clever ads for a product that didn't measure up. Virgin has seen its share of flops too. The heavily hyped Virgin Cola didn't last long in the United States, outgunned by far-more-entrenched rivals Coca-Cola and Pepsi. And Virgin Brides shuttered after nearly a decade, failing because customers weren't interested in a one-stop shop for bridal wear and wedding-planning services.

But Virgin Atlantic has been something altogether different. In 2009, as other carriers were bleeding money, Virgin grew its revenue and profits. At the same time, its archrival, British Airways, rang up its worst losses in more than two decades. Of course, design wasn't the only factor. Virgin aggressively cut prices, which helped it swipe share from other airlines. And a hedging strategy, by which the company purchased fuel two years in advance, shielded Virgin from the worst of the oil price surge in 2008.

These types of business strategies are helpful, but Branson remains convinced that design is the key to Virgin Atlantic's success. "The only reason the Virgin brand has survived so long is that people trust that the actual end products that they are going to get from Virgin are good ones," Branson says. When Virgin Atlantic made its maiden voyage back in 1984, its rivals included Pan Am, TWA, and British Caledonian. All of those airlines have long since faded away. And Branson is confident that his airline's focus on creating a great experience will help it outlast its current batch of competitors. "Some of these big American carriers have survived just because of their share dominance of the marketplace," Branson says. "But I think some of them won't survive much longer.

Virgin Atlantic is outlasting rivals because it isn't afraid to take chances in designing a superior customer experience. "One of my mottos is: Just screw it, let's do it," Branson says. He's adamant that success comes from trusting instincts and taking calculated risks. "If you ignore the accountants and you introduce stand-up bars, where people can get out of their seats and move around and talk to other people, if you do things like introduce masseuses onboard, if you introduce seat-back videos on economy class, yes, in the short-term, it costs more money," Branson says. "But in the long-term, the best always survive."

DESIGN IS HOW IT WORKS

9

THE
INTERSECTION
OF BUSINESS
AND DESIGN

I'm sitting in on a series of business presentations when Stephane Krumenacker takes the floor to pitch his idea for a new series of lighting products. Krumenacker, wearing blue jeans and a plain white T-shirt, is fresh-faced and clean-cut with big, bright eyes that suggest constant wonderment.

Krumenacker talks first about his target customers—young, active, urban shoppers who crave modernity. (Back when I was fresh-faced, we called them Yuppies.) His Power-Point presentation shows the likely haunts of the target market: sleek, modern condos and workplace cubicles. It features young folks eating food on the go, active twentysomethings at the gym or scaling a climbing wall. Krumenacker brings the focus back to the condo. "How can we bring an organic form of lighting into these little boxes in which people live?" he asks.

With his stage set, Krumenacker offers up sketches of

his potential products. First up, a floor lamp with multiple branches, each one with a different type of light, not unlike something you might find at IKEA. One has a heavy-duty bulb to light an entire room. Another is more of a book light. Then there's a branch with a cooler bulb for mood lighting.

His second product is a beanbag chair that lights up when someone sits on it. Novel, I think. And though decades separate me from his twentysomething target market, I can appreciate the potential appeal. That said, the old fart in me worries about the light dimming when I get up from the chair at night only to find that there's nothing else to light the way. But then Krumenacker wins me over with the addition of biometrics to change the color of the lighting based on a user's emotional state, sort of like a big, bean-filled mood ring.

His last offering: luminescent flooring that lights up as people walk on it. Each step creates a new light source that fades as the user moves forward. I like it. The middle-aged guy I am thinks that it would be nifty to have some low-intensity lighting guide my way in the middle of the night when I need to use the bathroom.

Krumenacker isn't talking to potential investors, and he's not trying to drum up media attention for his company. He's a senior at the Rhode Island School of Design, perhaps the nation's leading design school. RISD was founded in 1877 as a place for artists to improve their craft. Krumenacker is giving his midterm presentation for the Spirit of Product Design class. It's taught by Soojung Ham, a professor who has done design work for A. T. Cross Company, where she worked on the squat, barrel-shaped Ion pen that helped change the image of the stately pen maker. She also helped Gillette develop the $150 Fusion Chrome Collection Power Razor, sold at the company's tony Art of Shaving boutiques. Ham is the picture of the modern designer, wearing a black, long-sleeved T-shirt under her black blouse. Her long black skirt ends just above the black cloddy shoes that were once the favorite of workingmen. There's a tiny stud in her nose.

This is the day when her students give their midterm presentations, sketching out the product line they're going to pursue. There are fifteen or so in the class, crammed into a small room in an old six-story brick building that used to house a Scandinavian furniture store. It has a warehouse vibe; everything is exposed, from the ducts in the ceiling to the bricks in the wall to the hardwood floors underneath. To save space, students sit in chairs with desks attached, straight out of kindergarten. One of them is wearing a T-shirt that reads "Design will save the world." Prior to today's presentation, the students have done a fair amount of spadework, pondering where they think the market opportunity is, interviewing potential customers, scoping out the environments where they think their products will be used. It's a lot of business strategy for students who enrolled at RISD to perfect their art.

Ham is Krumenacker's first critic, and she's a little more cutting than I had expected. She says his products aren't really targeted to the young folks he mentioned as his potential customers. "It's a little open," Ham says. "It works for many people," not just the niche Krumenacker is hoping to sell to. The ideas are too general purpose. Interview potential customers, she advises, observe them as they go about their daily tasks. Then create a persona, a fictitious character in the target audience to help test the concept.

Ham is not entirely discouraging. She's enthusiastic about how Krumenacker's lights give users the ability to decide when and how to use them. "You do have control over the light, but it's not conscious," Ham says. She likes that users don't flip a switch to turn on the lights, but do so indirectly when they walk or sit on a beanbag chair.

In this book, you've read about how some of the world's most creative companies use design to thrive. Their cultures nurture design from the earliest stages of development through to the marketing and selling of the product. Nike's Tinker Hatfield spends days with Michael Jordan to find inspiration for the next Air Jordan shoe. REI's David Mydans sleeps in tents for one-sixth of the year to come up with his next breakthrough. Ace's Alex Calderwood trolls through consignment shops to find the perfect piece of macramé that creates a tone for his hotel.

But the vast majority of companies don't have design as a core competency. They are often stocked with number crunchers skilled at squeezing excess costs out of business processes. They have techno gurus who can conjure up cutting-edge gizmos. But they lack creative thinkers who are willing to listen to customers, watch their habits, and understand what they want, even if those customers don't quite know themselves what it is they are after. When they decide to march down the design path, they take half-steps, mimicking breakthroughs of rivals or adding a feature or two in the hopes that it will be enough to differentiate the product in a

194

crowded marketplace. All too often, they can't sustain innovation going forward.

Some of the smartest thinking about putting design at the core of business strategy is coming from academia. RISD, at the forefront of the revolution, hired graphic designer John Maeda away from MIT, where he served as the associate director of research at its Media Lab, in 2008. A rock star in the design world, Maeda also penned *The Laws of Simplicity*, a paean to keeping things simple in design, in business, and in life. He's transforming RISD, keeping the art culture, but infusing it with the knowledge of how design relates to business. "Everyone wants design. I've had it since 1877," Maeda says of his school.

So let's consider young Stephane Krumenacker and his lighting products once more. They show some imagination, though they're not likely to set the world on fire. But that's not the point here. Think about how he came up with his ideas. His first step was to think about customers. That was a good start, but all he really did was gather pictures of places where they live and work. He didn't spend much time trying to understand what their lighting needs might be. He just came up with some clever ideas.

No doubt Krumenacker is a bright young man. But he doesn't have the instinct that Clif Bar's Tom Richardson had in coming up with Shot Bloks. He's not as adept as Virgin Atlantic's Joe Ferry at creating an experience that customers crave. So Ham gave Krumenacker the tools to accomplish the same goals. She encouraged Krumenacker to become an ethnographer. Talk with twentysomethings to learn what kind of lighting they want, she said. Watch them use various types of lighting. Figure out what their unmet needs really are. Then Ham told Krumenacker to create personas to test his theories.

That's not the way businesses typically think about new products. More often than not, they start with a financial analysis of market segments. RISD wants its graduates to be the ones challenging convention at companies unaccustomed to taking risks. "You can be the subversive person on the team," Leslie Fontana, who runs RISD's industrial design department, likes to tell students. "There's that sense in people who have studied art to think beyond what's available. You're training yourself not to have constraints." That's important because incremental changes tend to come from executives unwilling to push boundaries. "The best product designs don't come from product research," Fontana says. "They come from interpreters, artists," people who can understand what consumers want before they know to ask for it. We've seen it time and again in the previous chapters.

The focus on the intersection of business and design isn't just happening at design schools. Business schools too are adapting to train tomorrow's executives to think like designers. That's because the most forward-thinking schools saw a change sweeping through the economy in the early days of the millennium, when all sorts of jobs shifted to India and Asia, forcing commoditization on a grand scale. Instead of growing profits by shaving costs, companies were forced to put more emphasis on innovation. The smartest business schools adapted, creating curriculums focused less on number

196

crunching and more on abstract thinking. Instead of nurturing the cold calculation of the left brain, they developed courses to cultivate the creativity of the right brain. Instead of teaching students how to react to market disruptions, they developed classes in how to create those disruptions.

There's probably no business school closer to the forefront of this shift than the University of Toronto's Rotman School of Management, and no academic pushing those boundaries harder that its dean, Roger Martin. He wrote one of the most important business books on the subject, *The Opposable Mind*, in 2007, and has turned the school into one of the leading testing grounds for his approach. Martin is the picture of the tweedy academic, even though he came to Rotman from a management consulting firm. What's left of Martin's hair is brown and gray. When we meet on a cool fall morning in Toronto, he's wearing an oatmeal-colored sweater with a quarter-zipper zipped up to the collar, gray slacks, and brown suede shoes. Like any good educator, he answers every question eagerly, with a zeal to inform and enlighten.

Martin believes that executives are often paralyzed by either-or solutions to business problems. That is, they look at a challenge and try to solve it with conventional strategies that come with trade-offs. A CEO might decide to cut costs, even though it means scaling back on innovation. Another might dial up the innovation meter, costs be damned.

In Martin's world, there's another way, something he's dubbed "integrative thinking," very similar to the Design Thinking mantra that IDEO's Tim Brown discussed in the first chapter. Martin postulates that if executives approach

197

problems the way designers do, with creativity that allows them to conjure up ideas not previously considered, they can have the best of both worlds. In his book, Martin describes the concept as "the ability to face constructively the tension of opposing ideas and, instead of choosing one at the expense of the other, generate a creative resolution of the tension in the form of a new idea that contains elements of the opposing ideas but is superior to each." It's a mouthful, but essentially Martin believes that if business executives think like designers, they can have their cake and eat it too.

That's not the tack business schools typically take in educating students. The *A* in MBA, after all, stands for administration. "Business education, to a great extent, has been about analyzing existing models," Martin says. "The people who have succeeded so brilliantly don't choose from models. They are creators and builders of new models. Business schools simply don't teach that."

Martin decided to test his theory back in 2003 at Rotman, offering an elective with the Ontario College of Art & Design where students from both schools created marketing campaigns for nonprofits. He wanted to give his students an education in coming up with novel strategies, not merely mimicking the successful tactics of others. It's the sort of abstract thinking design students learn. Within three years, he put integrative thinking at the core of Rotman's curriculum. "I'm going to bring the very best of design education into the business school world," Martin says. He's already turned it into one of the most highly regarded business schools in the world.

Teaching design to business students, though, doesn't

198

start with a blank sketchpad and an assignment to draw something from memory. In most cases, they won't ultimately be the ones who take molding clay and craft prototypes of future products. Instead, Rotman teaches them how designers approach problems creatively, experimenting with new approaches, accepting failure as a possible outcome and learning from it. They're taught how to use the mental tools of design to address business challenges.

One of the most innovative Rotman initiatives is Designworks, something of a laboratory where companies bring their problems to students to solve through integrative thinking. The students often start by trying to understand the needs of the end user, be it a customer, a patient, or a partner. It's a stage Designworks devotes to "empathy and deep-user understanding."

As obvious as this may sound, too often companies try to fit their business strategy around the breakthroughs from research and development or the needs of their annual business plan. They don't start with the basic question—what is it that consumers really want? That's often because it seems imponderable. So the students do a bit of cultural anthropology, interviewing customers and trying to understand their needs, even if the customers can't quite put them into words.

The next step, "concept visualization," uses this information to dream up products and services. But it's not about coming up with the one, perfect solution. The team develops several; the process of focusing on consumers often triggers a flood of ideas. Some of them are viable, others less so. Most won't become actual products, but the point is to imagine

199

the best products or services to meet the needs of customers, and then test those ideas. Often, they do this with rough prototypes, sometimes created with cardboard boxes and tape, just to see how their ideas might play out. Then they adjust based on that data. When they think they've hit upon something, the group works backward to figure out a way to create it with available technology, existing manufacturing processes, and within a budget. Or perhaps it requires rethinking those as well.

Once they've settled upon the approach, the group moves to the last step, figuring out if the product or service is financially viable. But "strategic business design," in the Designworks argot, isn't the traditional business school curriculum of number crunching. There is a certain amount of market research and finance that goes into it, to be sure. But remember, Rotman is trying to teach students to create new business models, not just emulate existing ones. Instead of plugging a new product into an existing business model, where the costs might easily kill the effort before it ever begins, the Designworks model calls for rethinking the entire process, considering ways to shave manufacturing costs, add new revenue streams from the business, and find possible synergies with existing product lines.

It's a bit like the business model around Nike+. Sure, there's some revenue to be made in selling the sensor that slips into Nike shoes. But the real business breakthrough was reversing Nike's market-share slide in those running shoes themselves. "Ultimately, it's about taking it to a new model," says Heather Fraser, the director of Designworks, who previ-

200

ously worked in research and business design at Procter & Gamble.

For most of the academics teaching the new approach, it's a near-religious quest. Nowhere is that more clear than at the Hasso Plattner Institute of Design at Stanford University. Better known as the d.school, it's a place where students learn Design Thinking from the folks who popularized the phrase among business types. Cofounded by David Kelley, chairman of IDEO, and the d.school's executive director, George Kembel, the school has a mission to create a new generation of innovators ready to step into a changing business world. It's also a place to proselytize Design Thinking, testing it in environments where design isn't common, such as philanthropy, hospitals, or radio. Kembel refers to it as "a movement."

The centerpiece of Design Thinking, as taught by the d.school, is harnessing the creativity sparked by smart people with different perspectives on the world. It wants business students to engage with design students and anthropologists, each sharing their expertise and learning from the specialties of the others. The belief is that from the collective comes insight that each group in its silo couldn't achieve on its own. "Design Thinking leads to a collaborative leadership model," Kembel says. That's one reason why the d.school's faculty comes from every corner of Stanford: educators from its business and engineering schools, computer science and medical professors, and those who teach psychology, anthropology, and art.

When I meet with Kembel, it's one of those warm fall afternoons that often grace Palo Alto. The long shadows cast by the autumn sun dapple Stanford's lush campus. It's already freezing in other parts of the country, but here, students cheerfully zip across the quad on bikes, wearing shorts and flip-flops as they make their way to class. The d.school has the feel of many of the Silicon Valley start-ups that make their home just down the road. It's a big, airy space, with loads of natural light and adjustable walls to fit the needs of the moment. There are smaller conference areas, such as the "Guru room," where teams can convene to map out strategies.

Like Rotman's Martin and Fraser, Kembel made his way to academia through industry. Before joining Stanford, he worked at a design consultancy and a software start-up. He has slid quite comfortably into his role at the d.school. Wearing a gray button-down shirt over a black T-shirt and black jeans, Kembel has little of his salt-and-pepper hair left on top, though he does sport a mustache and a goatee. He's animatedly discussing the mission of the d.school, standing more than sitting as he talks, scrawling diagrams of his thoughts on a whiteboard.

Despite its name, the d.school doesn't teach design and doesn't even offer degrees. Stanford already has a school where students study traditional product design. It also has separate schools where students can earn degrees in business administration, engineering, medicine, and a host of other disciplines. The d.school's students come from those other schools at Stanford, which confer degrees to them.

Like a lot of movements, Design Thinking has its share of buzzwords. One of the favorites at the d.school is teaching students to be "T-shaped." The vertical line of the *T* represents their area of expertise, be it a degree in medicine or finance or art. The horizontal line represents their ability to collaborate with others who have different areas of expertise. The goal is that a conference room full of T-shaped design thinkers can tap one another's areas of expertise, call on their own, and come up with insights at the intersections of all of their points of view.

"You've got to have variation," says Bob Sutton, a professor of organizational behavior at Stanford's Graduate School of Business and a d.school mainstay and author of *The No Asshole Rule: Building a Civilized Workplace and Surviving One That Isn't*. "You've got to be able to look at the same thing as everyone else and see things differently."

So how do they teach that? With classes such as Prototyping Organizational Change, where students apply Design Thinking to such mundane business practices as company-wide meetings, a process that could use a creative overhaul if ever there was one. They can also take the From Play to Innovation class, where they explore the importance that playfulness has in the process of creativity. Or they can sign up for the Creating Infectious Action class, where they study social movements and network theory to learn the art of creating large-scale persistent behavioral change.

So how do they do it? In late 2007, the über-hip messenger bag maker Timbuk2 was struggling with a crisis of culture. It had gone through change in ownership and strategy, including outsourcing warehouse operations from its San Francisco headquarters and adding new travel lines to its business. Some veteran staffers left while new business managers joined. Communication and trust had withered.

Then-CEO Perry Klebahn, who also taught at the

d.school, met with Sutton to discuss the problems. Sutton asked about Timbuk2's all-company meetings. "I said, 'They suck,'" Klebahn recalls. Not great for the company, but perfect for a two-week d.school project. A few months later, Sutton's students sat in on one of Timbuk2's weekly all-employee meetings. They found the company's seventy employees crammed into the company's harshly lit kitchen area, some standing and others crouching on the floor. Managers went down a laundry list of agenda items, keeping employees up to speed on changes in the business. There was little give-and-take. There was even less enthusiasm.

The students stuck around after the meeting, interviewing any employees willing to give a piece of their minds. They learned that employees didn't really know one another very well, with so many changes in recent months. They were proud of the company but insecure in their jobs.

From their observations and interviews, the students created prototype meetings. In a room at the d.school, they brought in sofas. They tinkered with lighting, even going so far as to try a meeting lit by candles. And they suggested warm-up exercises, where employees shared details about themselves before the business of the meeting began. Then, they brought a handful of Timbuk2 executives and staffers to Palo Alto to role-play in a handful of meetings, running through different scenarios to see what might work.

Of course, that's exactly how smart companies prototype products. Think back to the innovation processes at LEGO and OXO. They interview and observe customers. They mock up quick models, often veering toward the extreme to see what might work and what might not. Then, they test

204

their ideas and refine them. The d.school is using the same methods to create organizational change.

So what happened at Timbuk2? Klebahn instituted several of the suggestions. The meetings moved to Timbuk2's lobby, where there was more seating and more pleasant lighting. To celebrate Timbuk2's creative culture, the company gave one randomly selected worker a custom-made Timbuk2 bag designed to reflect his or her personality and interests. And employees began every meeting answering a question—what did you have for breakfast or what is the name of the first person you kissed? Employees began to open up. "It got us to know each other. It worked great," Klebahn says.

But actually creating large-scale behavioral change isn't really the goal. It's great when that happens, as it did with Timbuk2. But Sutton, Kembel, and the rest of the d.school use the classes to change the way students approach problems. "The focus is first on the transformation of the person, and second on the outcome of their work," Kembel says. "They are graded on process and outcomes."

Executives often fret about not getting the most out of their staff, about their not being efficient, about employees not feeling enthusiastic about their work. Design Thinking can be the antidote to that ailment. "People who are creative are walking around feeling not creative," Kembel says. They're shut down, discouraged from taking chances, trying new approaches, experimenting with novel ideas, because it's not their area of expertise. Worse still, those sparks of creativity are never even lit because workers live in a vacuum of similar-thinking colleagues. The d.school, Rotman, and

205

RISD all teach students to take the path less traveled, even if it means failing now and again.

"Trying things that might not work because it's a faster way to see what might actually work," Kembel says—"that's what we need to nurture in people."

206

Conclusion

IDEO's Tim Brown is a fan of Apple, but not for the reasons you might think. As the head of one of the most important design firms in the world, Brown appreciates a well-crafted product as much as anyone. He's helped design products for such companies as electronics giant Motorola and furniture maker Steelcase. And his work has been exhibited at the Museum of Modern Art in New York, the Axis Gallery in Tokyo, and the Design Museum in London. "One of the great things that Apple has done," Brown starts to tell me, "is getting industrial design out of the way and letting the experience take over."

Apple's crack staff of industrial designers spent months crafting the iPhone's minimalist, modern feel. It's sleek and trim and absolutely symmetrical. The face is a seamless pane of glass, framed by a chrome border. And it has only one button on the front, unlike any other phone that came before it.

Most owners, me included, would tell you that it's a thing of beauty.

And yet a leading industrial designer of the day celebrates the fact that the iPhone's success really has little to do with its aesthetics. The great breakthrough of the iPhone is what it does, not how it looks. It's all those cool applications that users can put on their phones, creating the precise experience they want.

These days, CEOs have their hands full. As I write this final chapter, the global recession that has stretched into 2010 shows signs of abating. But no one expects the recovery to be anything but slow. Businesses are shuttering. Workers continue to be laid off. Pricing pressure mounts. The idea of spending money on design to create experiences that consumers crave may seem like an unaffordable luxury.

Yet design, more than ever, is what will distinguish companies in the twenty-first century. Think about how LEGO used design to revive its City line, renew its Mindstorms business, and launch its Architecture models. It helped the company post double-digit gains in the depths of the recession. Ace Hotels was able to challenge established giants and trendy boutiques using design to carve a niche for itself. Nike gave runners an experience they never knew they wanted with Nike+ and reversed its slide in its running shoe business.

Experiences matter, and design can guide companies to create the ones consumers want most. One of the best places to learn how to create them is IDEO. To many, it's the church of Design Thinking, where the best ideas for new products, services, and business ideas are born. If that's the case, Brown is that church's high priest. A Brit, Brown took the reigns in

2000. IDEO was already a very good design firm back then, a place where some of the world's best-known companies came with clever technology but unformed ideas of how to present and package it. IDEO put the sheen on everything from a stand-up Crest toothpaste tube for Procter & Gamble to a portable defibrillator for Heartstream, and from the Palm V PDA to Steelcase's Leap chair.

Brown hasn't turned his back on his roots as much as he's evolved his notion about the powers of design. Design Thinking puts IDEO at the very earliest stages of product development. Sometimes it happens without clients ever really expecting IDEO to dive so deep. When the world's largest bicycle components manufacturer, Shimano, asked IDEO to help it design a casual bike for wealthy baby boomers, the firm started by questioning whether the company was even looking at the right market. IDEO wondered if Shimano should target a much broader audience, and sent out behavioral scientists as well as marketers to figure out who the ideal customers were.

They interviewed people who hadn't ridden bikes in years to learn why they'd stopped. And they found that noncyclists were put off by just about everything about the sport. Riding on streets where cars buzz within inches of bikes terrified them. Shopping in stores that catered to hard-core cyclists intimidated them. But if Shimano could minimize those obstacles, IDEO found, there was a huge new market that had fond memories of pedaling around the neighborhood as kids. With a little prompting, they could be convinced to get back in the saddle. When Shimano launched its new Coasting bikes in 2007 with

209

manufacturing partners Trek, Raleigh, and Giant, they quickly sold out the roughly thirty thousand bikes produced. IDEO helped Shimano conceive the product, not just titivate an idea.

IDEO's headquarters have a bit of the Wonka Chocolate Factory feel. When guests arrive, they wait in an open-roofed, semienclosed yurt, something of a New Age conference room. At the center is a table made from sheets upon sheets of paper, like a huge, circular memo pad, with colored pencils in the center, encouraging visitors to draw, or jot down notes and observations. When I visit, there are a few horse drawings and greetings on the top sheet of the pad from Rachel and Yasmine.

A parade of young, enthusiastic workers in blue jeans and T-shirts streams past, sometimes with folks who must be clients because they're wearing suits. The buildings are full of open spaces where colleagues tinker, strategize, and collaborate. And along with pens and whiteboards, there are toys all over, gewgaws such as the IDEO-created Finger Blasters, foam rubber-band-powered rockets that whizz around the joint every so often.

It's a lovely spring day when I visit, so Brown invites me to IDEO's second-floor patio, rolls down the electronic awning, and settles into a lime-green chair. He's wearing a bold shirt with stripes of orange, blue, green, and white tucked into his blue jeans. His black, wing-tip oxford shoes seem conservative enough until you catch a glimpse of the colorfully striped socks that appear to match his shirt. His salt-and-pepper hair is cut short, his mustache and goatee are

210

trimmed close. And with the warm spring sun beating down, he's sporting classic Ray-Ban Wayfarer shades.

It seems a bit incongruous for a company that's elbowing its way into the buttoned-down, starched-shirt world of management consultancies such as McKinsey & Company. But increasingly, that's what IDEO has become. It continues to do traditional product design, but it's making its mark helping companies figure out how to change their organizational structure to better understand what their customers need. "A well-designed organizational process brings a company much closer to its customers," Brown says. "That can pay off in so many ways."

It starts at the cash register. Obviously, if consumers love a product, they'll buy it. But companies clever enough to get consumers to crave their products generate loyalty that goes far beyond a single purchase. The success of the iPod enhanced Apple's reputation so much that consumers started buying Apple's computers. And great design pays off in goodwill as well. When Apple's MobileMe e-mail service cratered during its 2008 launch, customers didn't bail on the company. They grumbled, to be sure, but they gave Apple a chance to fix the mess. That's what great design can do.

Though the process is never cut-and-dried, there are some frequently used paces that IDEO puts itself and its clients through as they begin the process of designing a product or service. It always starts with observation. But that's not hiding behind a two-way mirror, watching customers in a controlled environment. IDEO pairs its psychologists and anthropologists with clients to shadow customers or potential

211

customers as they use products or services in their daily lives. They interview both hard-core users and first-time dabblers to understand the extremes of problems both sets of consumers face. They try to teach company executives about empathy, to help them step back from their cloistered environment and get a feel for what their customers go through. When it wanted to give Shimano and its bike-making partners a sense of the awkwardness neophyte cyclists feel when they walk into bike shops, for example, IDEO sent the executives, who were all men, to buy cosmetics at Sephora. It opened some eyes.

Then it's time to brainstorm. IDEO and its clients take all the data they've gathered, all the market information available, and even all the technology that the client has to offer and start riffing. They come up with ideas for products and services, the wilder, the better, because those concepts are often the most sea-changing. The most important rule is that participants have to defer judgment. They can't shoot down an idea, only build upon it or come up with something else.

IDEO takes the best of those ideas and creates prototypes. But these aren't expensive, detailed models. The more polished a prototype is, the harder it is to change it because designers are more invested in the concept. These basic prototypes are created quickly—often, just like those by the students at the Rotman school, with cardboard and tape—to demonstrate ideas and experiences, not actual features and textures. With them, IDEO creates personas, likely customers of the product or service. And then it assigns folks in the room to play the various parts, using prototypes to think through how they will work and where the shortcomings might be.

Now it's time to refine those ideas. This is a different type

212

of brainstorming, a process that zeros in on the ideas that best solve the consumers' problems or meet their unspoken needs. It's when IDEO and its clients figure out the path to market. Often, it involves backtracking and prototyping all over again, perhaps a bit more detailed this time as they zero in on an idea. Often, they'll show those prototypes to consumers and learn some more. "A lot of companies go through the design process and say, 'We won't show it to customers until it's perfect,'" Brown says. "We'd argue that it won't be perfect until you show it to customers."

When the product is perfected and it goes to market, IDEO tells the story. You could call it marketing, and you wouldn't be wrong. But marketing is all too often misleading, hype-filled, and dishonest. Storytelling IDEO-style has to be authentic, true to the product and the process that created it. "Really clever marketing that doesn't include really great design is much harder to find these days," Brown says. "Consumers are getting much more savvy, more informed." They can see through propaganda. But that doesn't mean it can't be interesting.

Take Pangea Organics, a soap and cosmetics maker that uses only natural products. They were a tiny company whose packaging was more suited to farmers' markets than national retailers when they came to IDEO hoping to grow the business. The company and IDEO came up with a new soap box, an egg carton–like package embedded with seeds of plants such as basil or amaranth. Soak the boxes overnight, plant them, and watch the seeds sprout. It helped tell the earthy story of the brand in a clever and authentic way. It was good enough to land Pangea's soaps on the shelves of Whole

213

Foods Market. Sales soared from $250,000 in 2005 to $5.8 million in 2008. "It was a huge part of who we are today," says Pangea founder and chief executive Joshua Onysko. "What I learned from that process is process."

IDEO is hardly alone among design firms moving further up the development food chain. About seven hundred miles north, in Portland, Oregon, Ziba Design is pursuing a similar path. It's a cool October day when I sit down for lunch at the trendy Bluehour Restaurant in Portland's hip Pearl District, a few blocks from Ziba's headquarters, with its founder and president, Sohrab Vossoughi. Born in Tehran, Vossoughi emigrated to San Jose with his family in 1971, when he was fourteen. He went on to San Jose State University, where he earned a degree in industrial design in 1979 before joining Hewlett-Packard, where he worked on low-cost printers. He started consulting three years later, and founded Ziba, which means "beauty" in Farsi, in 1984. Since then, the firm has designed products as varied as ergonomic keyboards for Microsoft to easy-to-test smoke detectors for Coleman.

Those were all great products that helped Ziba's clients. But Vossoughi thought there was more to design than aesthetics. "I didn't start Ziba to make stuff," Vossoughi says. He wanted to create experiences that fueled customers' passions. Design offered the methodology to do that. "It's a great tool for understanding," Vossoughi says. "Design is the creative thinking process of delivering innovation."

These days, Vossoughi takes pride in Ziba's work designing linger-friendly branches for Portland-based Umpqua Bank. Most consumer bank branches are efficient and cold. They funnel customers to ATMs for deposits and withdrawals

214

or put them in front of a bulletproof-glass window to handle more complex transactions. Umpqua believed its business would grow if customers were encouraged to slow down a bit, hang out at the branch, and have conversations with its staff.

So, with help from Ziba, Umpqua reconsidered its branch design. It created something of a hotel lobby, where customers can chat in lounge chairs with financial planners. They're offered free coffee and wireless Internet access. But this wasn't just moving furniture around and changing the drapes. It was about using design to reflect the brand values of the bank. The result: The branch generated $1 million in deposits the first week it opened. The locations cost roughly the same amount to build as traditional bank branches, but they generate deposits and loan balances that are more than twice as large as those of competing branches. It's been so successful that the bank has rolled out the concept throughout its network.

IDEO, Ziba, and a handful of other firms have turned the design world on its head, changing the definition of the word. In their hands, design is much more than just making things aesthetically attractive. The most creative companies develop methods to do consistently innovative work. They apply the lessons of design to all sorts of businesses, even ones in industries that don't lend themselves to creating works of beauty.

Careful readers may have noticed that this book started with companies that made objets d'art: beautiful sports cars and fashionable shoes, products created with the traditional tools of design. As the book progressed, we moved from companies that design artifacts to ones that design

215

experiences. They create stores that shoppers don't want to leave or air travel that passengers love, not loathe. That's because design is about creating something customers crave. Design isn't just for companies that make clothes, consumer electronics, or cars. No matter how mundane the business, design can help.

The companies I've written about in this book instinctively do what IDEO and Ziba preach. LEGO observes its hard-core fan base to see what they're building and learn where the company can find new markets. Clif Bar brainstorms in the Mary Erickson Test Kitchen, concocting some off-the-wall creations to see what might be the next hit. REI turns its not completely formed ideas for store design into prototypes and tests them in the marketplace, tweaking things along the way to figure out what resonates best. And it would be hard to find a company better at storytelling than Nike, whose customers buy its shoes as much for what they represent as for what they do.

That's really the point of this book. Use it to find some inspiration. There are lessons to be learned from Nike's appreciation of pop culture, Porsche's worship of performance, OXO's embrace of Universal Design, and Ace's ability to create hipness on the cheap. There is much to be gained by understanding each company's approach to making great products and developing wonderful services. But copying any one company's approach won't work. There are too many variables. Your company, the industry it's in, the executives who work there, the corporate culture, are all inherently different from the examples in this book. As Rotman's Roger

216

Martin would say, don't copy someone else's model; come up with your own.

Think like a designer as you map out company strategy. Many of the companies that are stumbling today are the ones that haven't addressed the challenges of the economy creatively. They are the ones that raced down the commoditization pit, shaving costs to compete with rivals instead of adding value. They followed the path of least resistance, pursuing a strategy that was easy to emulate. But for every one of them that slips, there's an opportunity to rise above them. There's a chance to become the next Apple, Nike, or Virgin Atlantic.

Some people are wired like Nike's Tinker Hatfield, LEGO's Paal Smith-Meyer, or Clif Bar's Gary Erickson to instinctively design great customer experiences. Some need to hire folks such as Tim Brown or Sohrab Vossoughi to help guide them on the journey. Figure out which one you are, because your customers are waiting for you to give them what they want.

Acknowledgments

This book wouldn't exist if Tim Sullivan hadn't e-mailed me in 2008, when he was an editor at Portfolio, to see if I'd be interested in writing it. I can't express enough my gratitude to him for approaching me and trusting me to pull this thing off. I had never written a book before, yet Tim believed in me and worked with me to craft a proposal that's the basis of this one.

Tim left Portfolio just as I began work on the book, handing off the project to Dave Moldawer. Dave's enthusiasm picked up just where Tim's left off. Dave possesses two of the most important traits any writer can ask of an editor: insight and patience. He steered me in the right direction whenever I veered off course, and graciously held my hand as I meandered into the new world of book writing.

The origins of this book go back to an article I wrote for *BusinessWeek* about the design process at Bang & Olufsen.

That story was meticulously edited by my former colleague Bruce Nussbaum. It would be hard to find a greater champion of the importance of design as a business strategy than Bruce and I've been fortunate to be the beneficiary of his wisdom. I would also like to thank Steve Adler, the former *BusinessWeek* editor, who graciously agreed to give me a year off to report and write this book.

Jim Windolf and Steve Hamm were both brave enough to read through an early manuscript and offer valuable suggestions that improved this book immeasurably. They're both terrific writers. They're even better friends.

I am grateful to my friend and lawyer Jim Fowler, whose counsel came free even though his friendship has cost me a few lunches. I'm also indebted to Whit Leibow, another friend and lawyer, who set up my book-writing business as a legal entity. And my agent, Jim Levine, didn't just negotiate the contract for this book—he helped shape it, offering insight and encouragement as each chapter landed in his in-box.

There are so many family and friends who offered transportation and lodging, as well as terrific conversation, as I hopscotched across North America and Europe. In particular, I'd like to thank my brother Adam Greene, who chauffeured me up the East Coast and into Canada, during an early reporting trip. Who knew his MX-5 would be handier than his MFA? I am also grateful to my brother-in-law, Carl Howe, who gave me not just a bed to lay my head on in Los Angeles, but his car to get around in and his design sensibility to shape my thinking.

220   I'm also very appreciative of all the help and time executives, academics, designers, and, in particular, their endlessly accommodating public relations staffs gave me throughout

the reporting and writing. Many of them appear in this book. Many more don't. But all of their efforts contributed.

As I turn the last page of my first book, I can't help but be appreciative of my parents, who set me on this path decades earlier. My mom, Judith Greene, taught me many things in life, not the least important of which is that the verb "to be" takes the same case after as before. She gave me an appreciation for words, grammar, and writing that led to my career and ultimately this book. My dad, Robert Greene, is simply the hardest-working man I have ever known. His values are instilled in me, even if I'll never put in the hours that he always did.

One of the lessons of this book is to remain open-minded to new possibilities; another is to constantly question convention. My boys, Will and Sam, remind me of the importance of both those skills every day. I know they look up to me. I don't know if they appreciate how much I look up to them.

Last, I'll never quite be able to convey the appreciation I have for the support of my wife, Rochelle Howe. When we exchanged vows, there was nothing in there about reading the raw copy of my first book. But it was something she did without hesitation, and did with as keen an eye as I could ever have hoped. She never questioned my numerous reporting trips, even though she was on the hook for tending to all the important stuff in our lives while I was gone. And she tolerated the occasional late hours and grumpy moods that authorship can bring. It all falls under the heading of love, something she gives me in spades every day. I'm a fortunate man.

221

Further Reading

Branson, Sir Richard. *Business Stripped Bare: Adventures of a Global Entrepreneur.* London: Virgin Books, 2008.

———. *Screw It, Let's Do It: Lessons in Life.* London: Virgin Books, 2006.

Brown, Tim. *Change by Design: How Design Thinking Transforms Organizations and Inspires Innovation.* New York: HarperBusiness, 2009.

Brunner, Robert, and Stewart Emery, with Russ Hall. *Do You Matter? How Great Design Will Make People Love Your Company.* Upper Saddle River, NJ: FT Press, 2009.

Erickson, Gary, with Lois Lorentzen. *Raising the Bar: Integrity and Passion in Life and Business.* San Fransisco: Jossey-Bass, 2004.

Esslinger, Hartmut. *A Fine Line: How Design Strategies Are Shaping the Future of Business.* San Francisco: Jossey-Bass, 2009.

Humberg, Christian. *50 Years of the LEGO Brick.* Königswinter, Germany: Heel Verlag GmbH, 2008.

Katz, Donald. *Just Do It: The Nike Spirit in the Corporate World.* New York: Random House, 1994.

Kelley, Tom, with Jonathan Littman. *The Art of Innovation: Lessons in Creativity from IDEO, America's Leading Design Firm.* New York: Doubleday, 2001.

Leffingwell, Randy. *Porsche 911: Perfection by Design.* St. Paul, MN: Motorbooks, 2005.

Lidwell, William, and Gerry Manacsa. *Deconstructing Product Design: Exploring the Form, Function, Usability, Sustainability and Commercial Success of 100 Amazing Products.* Beverly, MA: Rockport Publishers, 2009.

Maeda, John. *The Laws of Simplicity: Design, Technology, Business, Life.* Cambridge, MA: The MIT Press, 2006.

Manning, Harvey. *REI: 50 Years of Climbing Together.* Seattle: Recreational Equipment Inc., 1988.

Martin, Roger L. *The Design of Business: Why Design Thinking Is the Next Competitive Advantage.* Boston: Harvard Business School Press, 2009.

———. *The Opposable Mind: How Successful Leaders Win Through Integrative Thinking.* Boston: Harvard Business School Press, 2007.

Moore, Kenny. *Bowerman and the Men of Oregon: The Story of Oregon's Legendary Coach and Nike's Cofounder.* Emmaus, PA: Rodale, 2006.

Pine II, B. Joseph, and James H. Gilmore. *The Experience Economy: Work Is Theatre & Every Business a Stage.* Boston: Harvard Business School Press, 1999.

———. *Authenticity: What Consumers Really Want.* Boston: Harvard Business School Press, 2007.

Pink, Daniel H. *A Whole New Mind: Why Right-Brainers Will Rule the Future.* New York: Riverhead Books, 2005.

Strasser, J. B., and Laurie Becklund. *Swoosh: The Unauthorized Story of Nike and the Men Who Played There.* New York: Harcourt Brace Jovanovich, 1991.

Whittaker, Jim. *A Life on the Edge: Memoirs of Everest and Beyond.* Seattle: Mountaineers Books, 1999.

224

FURTHER READING

Index

Page numbers in *italics* refer to photographs.

225

intersection of business and, 189–206

service, 176

Universal Design, 91, 92, 100, 105, 167, 216

Design Business Association, 178

Design Museum, 207

Designworks, 199–200

d.school (Hasso Plattner Institute of Design), 201–6

Duffy, Ian, 141

Dürheimer, Wolfgang, 28–29, 30, 32

Dwell, 151

E

Eastman Kodak, 8

empathy, 11, 199, 212

Erickson, Gary, 131–35, 140–45, 168, 175, 217

Erickson, Mary, 135

Esslinger, Hartmut, 10

F

Fairey, Shepard, 154

Farber, Betsey, 90, 91, 116

Farber, Sam, 90–92, 93, 105, 116

Federer, Roger, 48

Ferguson, Michelle, 136, 137, 138

Ferrari, 19

Ferry, Joe, 176–78, 180, 182, 195

Fontana, Leslie, 196

Form Co., 100, 103

Formosa, Dan, 92, 103

Fraser, Heather, 200–201, 202

frog design, 10, 13, 113

Frostenson, Day, 109, 122–23

Fujiwara, Hiroshi, 47

Fuller, Buckminster, 120

G

Galidor, 69–71, *70*, 72

Gensler, 123

GFI Development, 164, 166

Giant, 210

Gillette, 193

Gilmore, James H., 23

Goshima, Jun, 39

Gould, Georgia, 133, 138

Graves, Michael, 93

Griffey, Ken, Jr., 58

Gropius, Walter, 6–7

H

Habeler, Peter, 116

Ham, Soojung, 192–94, 195–96

Hamm, Mia, 58

Hasso Plattner Institute of Design (d.school), 201–6

Hatfield, Tinker, 47–50, 194, 217

Hayami, Hideyo, 90

Heartstream, 209

Heath, Jonathan, 158–59

Heathrow Airport, 171–72

Virgin Atlantic Clubhouse at, 172–73, *172*

Hecox, Evan, 164

Helen of Troy Limited, 92

Herrick, Doug, 155, 158, 160, 166, 168

Hewlett-Packard, 10

Hitler, Adolf, 23

I

I.D., 151, 178

ideation, 11, 76–77, 139

IDEO, 13–14, 197, 201, 207–16

IKEA, 7

iMac, 8

integrative thinking, 197–98

International Home and Housewares Show, 99

iPhone, 7, 8, 9, 11, 207–8

iPod, 3, 5, 8, 9, 211

Nike+ iPod Sport Kit, 50–53, *51*, 200, 208

227

228

230

University of Toronto, Rotman
School of Management at,
197, 198–200, 202, 205–6,
212, 216
user needs, understanding,
12, 199

V
Vans, 55
Vincent, Lanny, 134
Virgin America, 181–86
  first class/coach barrier
    redesigned by, 185–86
  food service of, 184–85
  Main Cabin Select seats of,
    185–86, *185*
Virgin Atlantic, 12, 169–88,
  195, 217
  Clubhouses of, 172–73, *172,*
    174, 181
  flat beds of, 176–79, *179,* 181
  lighting systems of, 180–81,
    182–83
  sense of humor of, 180, 183
Virgin Brides, 187
Virgin Cola, 187
Virgin USA, 182

Volkswagen, 23, 35–36
Vossoughi, Sohrab, 214, 217

W
Walker, Rob, 3
Wallpaper*, 151, 178
Walmart, 164
Weigel, Wade, 153–55,
  166–67
Wells, Adam, 182, 183, 185
Whittaker, Jim, 116–17, 122, 123
Whole Foods Market, 123,
  213–14
Wick, Brent, 157
Willemann, Morten Juel, 76,
  77–78
Williams, Jordan, 127
Witt, Larry, 104
Woods, Tiger, 58, 81

X
X Games, 54, 57
XTERRA World Championship, 134

Z
Ziba Design, 214–15, 216
Zobler, Andrew, 164, 166

231